INTO GOD

By the same author

THE WAY INTO GOD

HUMAN NEEDS IN MODERN SOCIETY
(with B. T. Reynolds)

INTO GOD

An Exercise in Contemplation

R. G. COULSON

R. G. Coulson

What ye hear in the ear,
proclaim upon the housetops.
MATT. 10. 27 R.V.

ISBN 0 9503505 1 6

First published 1956

Reprinted in 1981, by The Bocardo Press, Cowley, Oxford

Contents

Preface

THIS BOOK is a practical attempt to meet an increasingly urgent need. This need, the deepest of all human needs, is man's need for God. For reasons which will be sketched in the first chapter, interest in mysticism has been steadily reviving in the Western world since the end of the last century. This interest, which is highly significant, is increasingly reaching the degree of intensity at which it seeks translation into action.[1] The result is that experiments in meditation and contemplation are taking place today all over Britain and, to some extent, America on a scale which is not generally appreciated. Not even in the Churches. No Branch of the Church has so far taken formal note of the movement.

It is perhaps partly for this reason that the experimentation began under the influence of the Eastern religions. Since these are not strongly represented in the West, however, the experimentation has seldom been soundly based on any established tradition. The results have naturally been mixed. They have often been disastrous, often merely negative, and the best that can probably be said of them is that they represent stunted fruit.

But though the Churches have officially ignored the movement, it has attracted a number of clergy and lay church-people, certainly since the second World War. This is not to imply any criticism of the Churches. They are no doubt right to suspend judgement until it is clear whether this work is of men or of God.[2] The supposed spiritual depth of the East, or possibly simply novelty, may have been the first attraction in some cases for these churchpeople. Be that as it may, it could not be long before the interest in the contemplative life came to be seen as thoroughly Biblical. Some surprise has been expressed, indeed, that the Church has so widely departed from the Bible in this vital matter, at any rate since the seventeenth century. The result, anyhow, is that an unknown, but certainly considerable, number of groups is scattered throughout Britain practising various forms of meditation and contemplation.

[1] Acts 2. 37.

[2] Acts 5. 38, 39.

Many of these groups are struggling along without benefit of clergy and are led by some devoted layman. Or, significantly, by some laywoman. The first object of this book is to give such groups some systematic help which is *Biblical.*

Other groups are led by clergy, but are often without much vision of the significance of the work. Their method is usually based on some tradition in the Church rather than on the Bible. It tends to be seen as a way of 'filling the empty pews' in the parish church rather than as the beginnings of a great movement of the Holy Spirit. Thus it tends to accentuate rather than heal differences of churchmanship. The second object of this book is to point such groups to the Universal, the Biblical basis of what they are doing, and to open their eyes to the tremendous potentialities that lie hidden therein.

But, as was said earlier on, most of the experimentation is going on outside the Church. Without benefit, that is, not only of clergy, but of theology of any kind worth the name. The third object of this book is to fulfil this lack as far as possible, to give these seekers some notion of the potentialities of the Church they have left, and to call upon them for help in actualizing these potentialities.

The last object of this book may well be the most important one, at any rate from a practical point of view. This is to give all varieties of groups practising meditation or contemplation an opportunity to *dwell* upon and to *study* the essentials of what they are trying to do. It is, or should be, impossible to take notes on the addresses given by conductors of groups in the course of introducing the contemplative silences. Otherwise they would be lecturers, not conductors. The essentials of these addresses thus tend to be forgotten. Here part of what at least one conductor in Holy Orders regards as essential can be considered at leisure.

This summary of the book's objects makes it clear, of course, that the book is not intended for complete beginners in the supreme work of knowing God. It is meant, rather, for those who are ready to reach out consciously and deliberately for the ultimate purpose of the work, for the ultimate end of all human existence, indeed, union with God. It is in this sense that beginners are spoken of throughout the book.

If God is the supreme Reality, The All as well as the Source of

All, it is clear that union with God must be the highest purpose that man can conceive for himself. Its pursuit must therefore be, not only the greatest theoretical, but the greatest practical problem of human existence. The emphasis in this book is on the practical side of the problem. For this is the most crucial of all. This naturally determines the style of the whole approach adopted here. A remark or two on the subject may save misunderstanding and disappointment.

In the first place, this book makes no claim to be literature. It is written as far as possible as one might speak to a group of like-minded people. Italics take the place of elaborate language in trying to express, or rather hint at, the more recondite ideas. Anyone who has ever tried to express the deeper levels of spiritual experience has always realized the hopeless inadequacy of language for the purpose. Words seem as inadequate as garden tools for the repair of a watch. Hence the writer is constantly tempted to break into 'poetry', extravagant symbolism, or obscure abstractions. The temptation has been resisted here. The more tremendous the subject becomes, the more simply and soberly it is treated. This makes for clarity, accuracy and above all *practicability*. So the reader will not be bemused by words, thereby remaining a reader instead of becoming a doer.[1]

Secondly, this book makes no appeal to science or philosophy, at any rate of the conventional kind. Psychological notions, for instance, are as far as possible expressed in general terms. So they are more likely to be lived out and not merely thought about. Ethics play a very subordinate part in the system outlined here. Not because they are unimportant, but because the true aspirant to union with God takes them for granted. His aim is not moral but Divine activity. Nor is any attempt made to argue the logical, or any other, necessity for believing in God. That, also, is taken for granted. So to argue would imply that so-called unbelief is a valid alternative to belief. Which would be as absurd as regarding ignorance as a valid alternative to knowledge. Belief in God is impossible without knowledge. Just as unbelief is impossible with knowledge.

It follows from this that the glimpse of history in the Introduction is primarily deductive. Historical processes are inter-

[1] Jas. I. 23.

preted, that is to say, in the light of God as the ONE Who makes, upholds, redeems and gathers together again all things visible and invisible. Actually, of course, any writing of history is never a mere recital of strings of events, but also an arrangement of these in the light of some preconception believed to be fundamental.

It remains for the writer to acknowledge with deep gratitude all the help that has made the writing of this book possible. He is unable to do so in detail. For the experience with which this book is concerned owes something, under God, to so many other books the author has read, and to so many relationships he has entered into, that acknowledgment in detail is impossible. Yet the Bible, together with the means of entering into its all-inclusive meaning, must be acknowledged as pre-eminent among the books that have helped him. He is bound also to thank his wife, his two daughters, the members of all the contemplation groups he is trying to help, and all the other fellow-pilgrims *consciously* treading the Way into God in every Great Faith.

Stansted Rectory,
Sevenoaks,
Kent

R.G.C.

Introduction

The Vision of God in the Twentieth Century

[1]

IF THIS BOOK aims at starting the aspirant off on a systematic pursuit of union with God, its main subject must be changeless and eternal. And if the system is sound, its principles must be valid in any age. But 'time is the moving image of eternity', and a man starts his search for God in his own age. We shall therefore have to introduce the main subject of this book, the Eternal, with a brief review of the particular segment of the temporal in which we are embedded. Yet we shall understand that segment only in the Light of the Eternal. Our brief review of the temporal must therefore begin with an attempt to catch the Light of the Eternal.

'Our Lord Jesus Christ said: Hear O Israel, The Lord our God is One; and thou shalt love the Lord thy God with all thy heart, and with all thy soul, and with all thy mind, and with all thy strength. This is the great and first commandment. And the second is like, namely this: Thou shalt love thy neighbour as thyself. There is none other commandment greater than these. On these two commandments hang all the Law and the Prophets.'[1]

As these familiar words of the Lord tinkle past the ear, without perhaps greatly impressing us, we do well to dwell on them, so that their supremely important meaning may at least *begin* to sink into us. Each of us understands the word 'God' individually, no doubt. Whatever the word may mean to us, however, most of us will agree that in its highest significance it means the Supreme Reality, The All as well as the Source of All.[2] The first fact we gather from the Lord's Summary of the Law, therefore, is that

[1] Our Lord's Summary of the Law in the alternative order for the Holy Communion in the 1928 Prayer Book, drawn from Mark 12. 29, 30 and Matt. 22. 37–40, slightly modified so as to accord with the Revised Version.

[2] Eph. 4. 6.

The All as well as the Source of All is not a multiplicity, as it appears to be, but a Unity, or rather The One.

The next fact that emerges is that The One is not an impersonal IT, but personal. For however glibly one may talk of loving things, one can genuinely love only an entity that is personal. The number one, for instance, or the One Reality are hardly lovable in any normal sense. The next fact that emerges, in short, is that The One Who is The All, as well as the Source of All, is I AM. Which is precisely as the Old Testament puts it. Or rather, as God identifies Himself to the human understanding.[1]

Finally, the practical purpose of the two great Commandments comes home to us. It is more important to us human beings than any other that is conceivable. The Commandments reveal to us the surest and shortest way to salvation. One can hardly imagine a word whose sense has been more distorted and degraded than the word 'salvation'. Let us try to detach ourselves from all these not very inspiring impressions, and grasp the deepest and most comprehensive sense of the much abused word. In this sense salvation must mean deliverance from all possible sin, evil and suffering, including all that flows from the fact of human mortality. The two great Commandments thus show us the surest and shortest way how we, the imperfect, suffering, transient many may become changed into the likeness of the Supreme, Eternally Perfect One Who is above all, and through all, and in all. For it is a fact of human nature that it takes upon itself, inevitably, the likeness of that which it loves. And the deeper, that is to say, the more adoring, more worshipping, more self-forgetful that love is, the more rapidly and surely the transformation takes place.

The notion of change into the likeness of God is highly ambiguous. For if God is the Supreme Reality, The One Who is The All as well as the Source of All, there can obviously be nothing *like* God. There can, indeed, be nothing outside or beyond God to become like Him. To be changed into the likeness of God can therefore only mean to be transformed from, or rather, to be awakened from the human to the Divine State.[2]

The supreme significance and importance of the Lord's Summary of the Commandments thus becomes clear. He, Whom all spiritually most aware human beings have come to regard as The

[1] Exod. 3. 14. [2] Rom. 12. 2; Eph. 5. 14.

One Incarnate, really sums up for us the ultimate purpose of human existence, individually as well as collectively.[1] No purpose *can* be greater than to be changed from the limitations and miseries of a transient fragment into the Eternal Joy of the Perfect One Who is above all, and through all, and in all. Nor could any change be greater. For before the Perfect One the fragment is virtually nothing. The change from being *as* nothing to being The All is thus most justly called salvation. And the means to that change, the two great Commandments, are thus most rightly placed in the forefront of the Gospel of Salvation. While He Who brought the Gospel to mankind, demonstrated before human eyes the actual process of the change from the human into the Divine, and so in all senses made possible the impossible, is most truly called Saviour and Redeemer.

Does this view of the Gospel appear extravagant? Does it read too much into the Saviour's Summary of the Commandments? Some may even find the notion of the transformation of the human into the Divine preposterous, not to say blasphemous. Whoever feels any such doubts cannot know the Bible, least of all the New Testament. Space does not allow us to set out in full the Biblical authority for this view. The whole Bible is a progressively expanding exposition of this view, as well as a practical guide to the actual transformation which constitutes salvation. Let S. Paul represent the whole Bible on this subject. 'Our Lord Jesus Christ, though he was rich, yet for your sakes he became poor, that ye through his poverty might be rich.'[2] Irenaeus, a little later, expressed the same view even more directly. 'Our Lord Jesus Christ did through His transcendent love become what we are, that we might become what He is.' A little later still Athanasius expressed it still more directly. 'He was made man', he declares in his *De Incarnatione*,[3] 'that we might be made God.'

But there is no need for further argument to support the view of the Gospel here given. However one may regard the two great Sacraments in detail, in their deepest significance they can be nothing less than the means of man's union with God. What else,

[1] Jesus Christ is regarded as God Incarnate or as the Supremely Enlightened One in both Hinduism and Buddhism; though not of course uniquely so, or neither would still exist as separate faiths from Christianity.

[2] 2 Cor. 8. 9. ('that' omitted).

[3] 54. 3.

indeed, did the Lord institute them for? This is clear from the actual words in which He is recorded as having instituted the Sacraments. But nothing expresses His Gospel more clearly than His call to His disciples to be united with Him. 'Abide in me, and I in you.'[1] A more literal call to union with Himself can hardly be imagined. And, of course, the two Sacraments closely correspond with the Call. In Holy Baptism we are incorporated into Christ, and so come to abide in Him. And He comes to abide in us as we, verily and in truth, partake of His Body and Blood, that is to say, the Divine Nature and Life, in the Holy Communion.

And if anyone should still have doubts about the view of the Gospel here given, let him consider the Catechism in the Book of Common Prayer. The two Sacraments are expressly stated there to be 'necessary to salvation'. According to even the most conventional and generally accepted view, the whole purpose of religion is to 'save the soul'. There is no salvation apart from union with God. Any more than there is existence apart from being.

[2]

The Gospel Message, being what it is, is obviously supremely important for all mankind. The Message is of course not an exclusively Christian possession. The Message is necessarily the basis of all the great religions. Or they would be neither great nor influential. It is only in Christianity, however, that the Message is completed and fulfilled by the actual Incarnation of God at a certain time in history and in a certain point in space. This not to disparage the other great religions. It is only to mention the obvious fact that one of them must be the culminating point.

Since God has actually become incarnate, the connection between the Gospel Message and human well-being has become closer than ever. For there is now less justification for error than ever before, and the consequences of error very quickly become manifest. The more faithfully the Message is proclaimed and accepted, on the other hand, the better the ultimate purpose of human existence is understood and the more deeply human values, aspirations and institutions are thereby coloured. Man-

[1] John 15. 4.

kind, enlightened by the Vision of God, knows the Way (in all senses), and human history correspondingly records progress. Conversely, whenever the Vision of God grows dim, mankind loses the Way, and human progress falters. As always, of course, there is a time-lag between cause and effect varying in length according to local conditions of time and place. But that is a detail we need not consider here.

The longer mankind wanders, bereft of the Vision of God and ignorant of the Way into God, the more its difficulties accumulate. Its sufferings increase. Sooner or later this inevitably recalls mankind to a search for the Vision. For the search is analogous to the impulse to avoid pain on the biological level. On their widely different levels, both ultimately spring from the creaturely need for Being and Life, in other words, for Living Reality.

Inevitably, too, the search sooner or later leads to the rediscovery of the Vision of God.[1] Also of the Way into God. The inevitable occurs simply because ultimately there is only one Living Reality. The search is therefore bound to go on until not only the one Truth and one Life, but one Way, has once more been found. All wrong turnings are ultimately barred by suffering. Entire civilizations may of course perish in the course of the search. The decay of civilizations bereft of the Vision of God may even be a necessary prelude to success in the search. But sooner or later success is inevitable. Then a new age of faith dawns, and mankind once more resumes its progress along the Way into God, the Living Reality.

Each age rediscovers The Way in its own terms. The Rediscovery, at the time it is made, therefore appears as a new discovery. Many generations may pass before the discovery is recognized to be a rediscovery. A synthesis between the new and the old then occurs. It is this dialectical, ever-richer realization of the Supreme Reality, and entry into It, or rather Him, which constitutes the overall progress of mankind.

Because human progress is inevitable, however, it is certainly not automatic, as the nineteenth century is said to have imagined. For each return to the Way, each step forward along the Way, is won only at the cost of incalculable suffering, aspiration and inspired endeavour. But progress is ultimately inevitable, and

[1] Matt. 7. 7.

reason forbids us to doubt this. A review of history from below, from the biological point of view, as ours has so far been, already makes this obvious. When viewed from above, from the Divine 'point of view', no doubt whatever is possible. Not possible, of course, to those who are aware of the Divine point of view, if only at second hand, 'from books'. For God is Love. Being Love, God wills the salvation of mankind.[1] Being Almighty, God's Will cannot ultimately be thwarted. As all the great religions testify, therefore, whenever mankind loses the Way into God and jeopardizes its salvation, God visits His beloved and sets the blundering, purblind creature upon its way once more.

Since the Incarnation, however, doubt is no longer merely impossible. It is not strictly conceivable. Again, of course, for those who even dimly perceive the purpose of the Incarnation. For man actually *has found* his Way into God and completed the journey, through Christ. In Jesus Christ God actually *has* reconciled or reunited man with Himself.[2] Man *is* in God through Christ. His life *is* hid with Christ in God.[3] However long the tail of the column may take to reach its Goal, the end of the journey must come for all, and in a sense already has come, because the Head is there.[4]

[3]

Having noted the rhythm, the pulse of the human struggle for the attainment of the ultimate purpose of human existence, we must now glance at the latest instance of this rhythm, the one in which we ourselves are involved in the twentieth century. Unfortunately space allows us only to note the barest essentials of a fascinating and extremely complex subject. And even then only in the most general terms.

It is customary to speak of the Mediaeval period as the last great Age of Faith, at any rate in the West. Whatever this may mean exactly, there is no doubt that mediaeval man had a more or less clear notion of the purpose of human existence. The Age began with a great intensification of the contemplative life as part of the search for the Vision of God after the miseries of the Dark Ages. The contemplative life as a general rule only flourished

[1] 1 Tim. 2. 4.
[2] Cor. 5. 18.
[3] Col. 3. 3.
[4] Col. 1. 18.

in monastic seclusion. But in due course the more or less conscious pursuit of union with God in the enclosed orders became reflected in secular society in the usual appropriately diluted form. One may say that the contemplative's interest in the Way *into* God became reflected in the worldling's interest in the Way *to* God. The Commandments were of course broken as much as ever. But most men had at least some notion, however nebulous, of God as the Supreme Reality, as well as of the ultimate purpose of human existence. It is irrelevant that these notions were often given an *expression* which, to us, seems childish, fantastic or preposterous.

Such a comparatively integral outlook upon human existence, with its freedom from doubt and interior conflict, naturally led to a great liberation of vitality. The result was the manifestation of self-consciousness, and all the experimentation and adventure this led to, from empirical science to voyages of discovery, which is called the High Renaissance. An Age of Faith thus bore fruit as an Age of Progress.

Progress, however, led mankind into the usual dangers. Drunk with success, Renaissance man forgot the source of his successful progress.[1] Exuberantly leaping into the place of God as the centre of interest, adolescently self-reliant, he made himself 'the measure of all things'. It would be interesting to review the number of times the Bible records warnings against this danger.[2] On this occasion, however, even those responsible for uttering the perennial warning to their own generation lost their sense of proportion. The fifteenth-century Papacy seems hardly credible to-day. The Reformation and Counter-Reformation certainly marked a revival of the Church's Vision of God, as the crop of mystics and saints of the period testify. But Renaissance man's self-consciousness had developed too fast and far for him to heed the dangers of uncontrolled and unmitigated humanism. Sweeping the Church along in his wake, he perverted her from the Ideal she was in the world to proclaim and pursue.

Nothing marks the decay of the Vision of God and the advance of spiritual myopia more clearly than the decline of true, practical mysticism from the end of the seventeenth century onwards. In the eighteenth and nineteenth centuries the ideal of union with

[1] *Cf.* Deut. 8. 11. [2] *E.g.* Deut. 6. 10–12.

God became hardly more than a metaphor, even for most of the priesthood. Inevitably, first religion, then its fruit Christian ethics, began to lose their point, and therefore to decay. During the nineteenth century both still to some extent mitigated the disruptive effect of self-consciousness in the raw, but as fashion and custom rather than as religion and ethics. By the beginning of the twentieth century their mitigating power had declined to the flash point of the first World War.[1]

With the first World War the progress ushered in with the Renaissance came to a stop and became a regress. The revolutions throughout Europe which followed the first World War shattered the established social pattern, and with it the religious and ethical customs guiding the masses. There was little now to oppose the complete secularization of the values, aspirations and institutions of Western society. There was nothing any longer *fruitfully* to mitigate the disintegrating effect of self-consciousness. The second World War marked a further stage in the regress, and the uneasy situation which has followed has disclosed the unsuspected ease and speed with which civilization is crumbling. The possibility of a third World War, and the methods with which it is likely to be waged, implies the shape and period of final collapse.

This war may of course be staved off for some time. It may even be avoided altogether. For a third World War would merely be a particularly violent form of a general state of disharmony which is inevitable once the inspiring, unifying and restraining Vision of God has been lost. It is this loss which is the underlying cause of the collapse. Just as the resulting conflict and disharmony are superficial causes. When we consider the all-pervading effects of disharmony between individuals, between social groups, between nations and groups of nations, we realize that here *is* collapse. It is hard to say whether unrestrained self-consciousness, or the attempts to restrain self-consciousness by dictatorship, are destroying the present order of civilization more effectively. One is almost tempted to regard a third World War as a merciful release, literally as a *coup de grâce*.

[1] Someone familiar with Christianity in Britain may object that this gloomy picture entirely omits such signs of religious vitality as the Evangelical and Tractarian Revivals and the great missionary activity of the period. But, briefly, these movements cannot have represented great spiritual vitality since religion lost its influence so soon afterwards.

Some may regard this as not only gloomy, but perniciously fatalistic pessimism. If there is really no hope of averting the coming collapse of civilization, why raise the distressing subject at all?

The answer is that it is only for the *present order* of civilization that there is no hope. For it has become detached from its spiritual foundations, from the Divine Ground, and, like an uprooted plant, must die. How soon the new order, the new plant, will grow up out of the decaying old depends entirely upon the rediscovery of the ideal of union with God.

[4]

The uncertainty, frustration and often despair which have grown up since 1914, and the prospect of incalculably greater suffering which has opened up since 1945, however, have begun to produce the inevitable result. Disillusioned with human resources, the most intelligent and sensitive human beings are once more trying to see beyond the human level. We see this clearly both within and without the Church.

Let us glance first at the Church. Many Branches of the Church have gone through a more or less public self-examination, and are more or less conscious of infection with secularism and humanism, and of the loss of the Vision of God. Prayer in its widest and deepest sense is once more *genuinely* beginning to be seen as the key to the Church's spiritual power. Above all, union with God is once more coming to be recognized as the supreme practical ideal for human beings, and not merely as a beautiful metaphor.

So far this ideal merely interests theoretically, on the whole. But there is no doubt that there is also a stirring of interest in the contemplative life as a means of actually pursuing the ideal and of attaining union with God. The mediaeval Church grasped the ideal more clearly, and was more experienced in the pursuit of its attainment than at any other time since then. Hence the contemplative life is usually seen in the traditional terms of the enclosed orders. But those who are seriously drawn to the contemplative life are not always able to enter such orders. A fairly common compromise is to follow some system of spiritual exercises associated with one of the active orders, such as the Ignatian method. The compromise may suit some aspirants to union with God. But it by no means suits all. In any case, no compromise is more than a *pis aller* in the spiritual life. Furthermore, such methods often represent a considerable departure from Biblical simplicity. For this reason, above all, we cannot be satisfied with them.

Let us next glance at the situation outside the Church. The disillusionment with human resources is even more clearly apparent outside the Church. Members of the Church are always liable to be lulled into complacency. 'Abraham is our father.'[1] They are sheltered from the misery of total ignorance of God. Hungry though they may be, they are not wholly starving. But outside the Church there is no shelter from the empty purposelessness of existence. One result is the renewed interest in religion among some artists, scientists and philosophers. The last two or three generations of these modern leaders of Western society have regarded themselves as the new priesthood of a new religion. In the middle of the twentieth century something of the depth, comprehensiveness and integrality of *true* religion, as apart from what the Church has so often propagated in recent centuries, is being borne in upon them. As yet they seldom abandon their secular outlook. They are prepared nevertheless to find 'something in religion'.

A deeper sign of interest in religion is the growing appreciation of mystical poetry and theology. But the deepest sign of all is the growing experimentation with various forms of yoga and contemplative exercises, usually among intelligent people who are neither specifically artists, scientists nor philosophers but sincere spiritual seekers, who in other times would have been among the backbone of active churchpeople.

One may be tempted to deduce the revived interest in religion outside the Church from the revived ideal of Union with God within the Church. It seems reasonable to suppose that to the extent that the Church represents true religion, she must inevitably begin to attract society as a whole. The facts, however, speak differently. As the Church has itself frankly declared, Christ attracts, but the Church repels.[2] Seekers outside the Church seem to

[1] John 8. 39.
[2] The Report of the Archbishops' Commission on Evangelism, 1945.

associate neither the religion nor the mysticism they are attracted to with the Church. Hence they seldom look to the Church to satisfy their growing hunger and aspirations. They identify the Church with the old form of religion. And they regard both as dead.

The Church naturally does not take kindly to this, and tends to condemn the spiritual aspirations of those outside as dilettantism, or worse. The two symptoms of spiritual revival, within and without the Church, thus seem to have appeared side by side without any definite link between them.

What is the reason for this co-existence? There can only be one satisfactory answer. The revived interest in the ideal of union with God both within and without the Church is nothing less than the movement of the Holy Spirit of God Himself. For God is Love, and wills all men to be saved. So God once more visits mankind and guides it back to The Way it has lost.

[5]

Because the Holy Spirit is moving both within and without the Church, one may feel tempted to accept this duality without question. Who is man, after all, to question the ways of God? But on reflection it becomes clear that the duality originates, not from God, but from man. God is the Eternal, Perfect One, and His Divine movement must therefore be eternally and perfectly integral. The apparent duality of His movement in the twentieth century must therefore be due to society's inability to apprehend and manifest His movement in a more integral manner. This inability becomes obvious to anyone detached enough to view all contemporary society, including the Church *Militant*, not as an end in itself, but as a phase of man's ascent to union with God. One so detached sees the reasons for the duality of the search for God within and without the Church. He appreciates, further, that the search along two unconnected paths is defective and cannot be truly fruitful until both unite.

We need not here embark upon a review of all the defects. Nor need we estimate whether the search for God within or without the Church is the more promising. All we need do is to note very briefly, but clearly, exactly why the search within and without the

Church, in separation, cannot be truly fruitful. Both must unite to be fruitful.

Let us begin with a glance at the Church. The search within the Church enjoys the enormous advantage of 'sound doctrine'. Those who are rediscovering the contemplative life within the Church can draw upon the vast storehouse of tradition embodying nearly two thousand years of experience. The Way into God is soundly mapped out for them, not only as regards theory (theology), but as regards practice (method). But the traditional map has its peculiar dangers. Tradition invites repose upon past achievements, and as we have seen, induces complacency. Supreme endeavour, without which man's supreme destiny cannot be fulfilled, is liable to wilt in such an atmosphere. The terms in which the map is drawn speak to the mind of the past rather than of today, still less of tomorrow. The psychology, the illustrations, the whole context of the traditional way is thus liable to appear irrelevant to the problems of the twentieth century. Lastly and more importantly, tradition implies that the contemplative life, and especially the aspiration to union with God, is within the reach only of the celibate in cloistered seclusion. The secular clergy, that is the great bulk of the Christian Ministry, may thus fail to hear any call to union with God. Lay churchpeople must feel altogether excluded from the Call.

Now let us turn to the search outside the Church. This enjoys the enormous advantage of freedom. The search beckons as the supreme personal adventure, tapping the deepest springs of endeavour. But therein lie great dangers. From the start sound doctrine tends to get impatiently pushed aside as pedantry. The aspirant thus begins his ascent to union with God without any soundly prepared map. Often without any map at all. He starts practising spiritual exercises, rushing to get on, and rushes in where experienced contemplatives fear to tread. He brushes aside all warnings and offers of guidance as attempts by ecclesiastics to maintain their dwindling authority. He grossly underestimates the hardships of the Way into God, and is usually quite unaware of its dangers. Because all human beings are called to union with God, he assumes that all are fit to *enter* upon the Way regardless of their existing state. Hence he sets out, unpurged and undedicated. The result is that the high adventure almost inevitably ends either in failure (the seeker fails to find) or in disaster (the seeker destroys himself mentally, morally or spiritually). But even if he accidentally stumbles upon the true Way into God, he probably finds himself travelling alone, or at best with a small group. He is thus without the fellowship of the great pilgrimage into God, past, present and future. And any contribution he or his group might make to the pilgrimage is lost.

[6]

This review, brief as it is, should make it clear why pursuit of the Way into God within and without the Church must unite. The pursuit cannot prosper unless it rests on the full Christian tradition, yet is freely undertaken as the supreme liberating adventure open to mankind. Christianity itself springs from a marriage of these apparent opposites. Jesus Christ proclaimed the Gospel to the Jews steeped in the tradition of Judaism. Yet His message was so inspiring that He was destroyed as a dangerous revolutionary. How could it be otherwise, indeed? How could the Way into God demand anything less than the resources of the whole personality? Union with God would be something less than the supreme destiny of man if it failed to tax to the uttermost the human mind, heart and will, united in the pursuit of a single sovereign purpose.

What does all this mean in practice? How is the traditional conception of the Way into God in cloistered celibacy to be combined with the unfettered search for the Way outside the Church? It is as easy to give the answer as it is difficult to put it into practice. Men and women *in the world* must embark upon the contemplative life with the same devotion and intensity as it was formerly pursued in cloistered seclusion. The next great Age of Faith, as well as the next great Age of Progress towards the fulfilment of man's destiny, cannot begin until this takes place.

Innumerable objections immediately suggest themselves. Most of them can probably be summed up as follows. One who is in the world, earning a living and raising a family, simply has neither the time nor the seclusion, nor the freedom from distractions to pursue the contemplative life with the same devotion and intensity as the 'religious'. What is possible *out* of the world is not possible *in* the world, simply because the world is what it is.

The objection is valid *in the world of to-day*. But if the matter is left there, then no age of faith will ever begin, and no age of progress will follow. The world will never be fit for another great step in the ascent into God. On the contrary, the rapid decay of the present order of civilization warns us that the world is rapidly becoming less and less fit for this. It is clear that a beginning must be made as soon as possible to found a new order of civilization which, because it subserves the human ascent into God, is viable. And that beginning can only be made by those who are determined to attempt that which is commonly judged to be impossible. This is to seek union with God in the world with the same intensity and devotion as it was formerly sought out of the world. Their devotion alone can change the world and fit it for a general advance of mankind.

No one who even faintly appreciates the difficulty of such an undertaking will, of course, expect to catch up his mediaeval predecessors quickly. Where the latter made a clean break with the world, the modern aspirant to union with God will have to disentangle himself from it by slow and painful degrees. Where his predecessor was free to devote himself to the fulfilment of his life's purpose without the least distraction, he will have to carve his freedom out of a working day teeming with calls on his mental, emotional and volitional resources. His devotion will therefore be far more severely tested than his predecessor's. So much so, indeed, that he may well regard the test as impossibly severe.

There is only one solution. 'All things are possible to him that believeth.'[1] As this book will clearly show in later chapters, by faith we come to discover that all impossibilities are no more than apparent. And we seek the faith that overcomes impossibilities in the degree that our need drives us to do so.[2] When the present order of civilization has decayed far enough, many will seek that faith. For the alternative will be despair and perhaps suicide. This book is intended for those who already foresee the ineluctable choice.

One more doubt perhaps needs to be dealt with. If the situation is as desperate as is made out here, why seek untried ways of retrieving it, especially ways that are so much more difficult than

[1] Mark 9. 23. [2] 1 John 5. 4.

the traditional ones? But the plain fact is that the traditional ways do not inspire many of those who are most actively groping for union with God. Or they would not be outside the Church.

But in the last resort there is another and a far deeper reason why the ascent into God must be pursued in the world rather than in monastic seclusion. As we saw in section 2, one day the tail of the column must follow its Head into God. Sooner or later all mankind must become reunited with God. 'As I live, saith the Lord, every knee shall bow to me, and every tongue shall confess to God.'[1] In the dispensation of the fullness of times all things shall be gathered together in one.[2] The day will dawn when 'we all come . . . unto a perfect man, unto the measure of the stature of the fullness of Christ'.[3] How are *all* to come to that day if they can only do so in monastic seclusion?

The monk may still reply that those who follow him will alone come to that blessed day, if only one by one. But Jesus Christ demonstrated the ascent into God in the world, not in seclusion. And He chose His followers from among the common people of the world. There are therefore no sound reasons why His call to abide in Him should not be heeded today in the world. On the contrary, the gathering of *all* things into One leaps forward in those who do.

[1] Rom. 14. 11. [2] Eph. 1. 10. [3] Eph. 4. 13.

Chapter One

To whom this book is addressed

[1]

WHOEVER has come with us so far, and understands the promise enshrined in the Gospel, must agree that a beginning will have to be made in seeking union with God in the world *some* day. But he may still doubt whether the mid-twentieth century is the day for this beginning. The Way into God is traditionally taught only by personal contact with those fit for it. 'Give not that which is holy unto the dogs.'[1] The mere publication of a book on the subject therefore seems to imply that the day has not yet come. Can any system of spiritual exercises which is offered to all and sundry, as it must be in a published book, really be sound? Have we not here yet another 'system of yoga', another amateur effort seldom conspicuous for soundness?

The last question is really the best proof that the day has come. For unsound systems appear largely because sound ones suitable for the contemporary mind are scarce. This book thus aims at outlining a Way into God which suits at least some contemporary minds, as experience has proved, yet which never for a moment departs in any essential either from the Bible, or from the great Christian Tradition.

But however much this needs publishing in the mid-twentieth century, it must still as far as possible be kept from falling into unsuitable hands. The best solution of the difficulty is to outline a few salient features which anyone ready to attempt The Way as set out here must recognize in himself. If he does, let him proceed. If not, it would be best to delay. There is no particular significance in the order in which these features are set out.

There is one safeguard against serious abuse of the system outlined here, in any case, which is final. The system, being Biblical, involves too much hard and painful work. The power this leads to is received only as the desire to *abuse* it is lost.

[1] Matt. 7. 6.

[2]

The first feature is obvious. It is general agreement with the Introduction's diagnosis of mankind's gathering difficulties and with the way out of them suggested there as the only possible one. It is so important to see the situation quite clearly that an outstanding point may with advantage be emphasized here and there.

We begin by clearly recognizing that by the twentieth century Western society has lost the ideal of union with God and is ignorant of the supreme purpose of human existence. Being at the head of man's development to self-consciousness in the mass, as is proved by the adoption of his values throughout the world, Western man is thus leading the whole human race into increasingly disastrous difficulties. The Way into God lies only through the Universal Church. Yet unless he recognizes The Way as a challenge to his whole personality, as the supreme personal adventure open to man which rouses all his zest, he will not enter upon it. He certainly cannot advance upon it. For man's supreme destiny can only be fulfilled through man's supreme endeavour. God's call to union with God is worthy of nothing less.

So far this merely recapitulates the Introduction. We now have to enlarge a point. From all that has been said it is clear that, if the search for union with God within and without the Church is to unite, the Church will have to modify her traditional conception of the Way into God. We now have to ask which Branch of the Church is most capable of reform and of performing the great task of leading mankind back upon the Way into God.

Humility and tolerance, if genuine, usually indicate strength, life and health in individuals or institutions. No Branch of the Church is more truly humble and tolerant than the Anglican. It therefore seems at least as capable of reform as any other Branch of the Church. Its potential capacity to lead the whole human race back upon the Way, however, seems unique. It is the established church of one of the politically most mature and socially most integrated nations on earth. No nation seems better fitted to guide mankind towards permanent political unity. (The British Commonwealth of Nations may be the seed of this already.) Its established church, reformed and purified by the coming suffering, thus seems fitted to become the truly Universal, truly Catholic Church. That Catholicity will be real, not nominal; inclusive, not exclusive.

Anyone who knows the Church of England today may well be excused for asking for evidence in support of these great claims. The only (possibly cryptic) answer one can give here is that it is necessary to live in the country to see the promise of the oak in the acorn.

Such a view of the Church of England might suggest that this book is mainly addressed to Anglicans. But it is not addressed to them alone. Or all those seeking union with God in other Branches of the Church would be excluded. So would all those who belong to no Branch of the Church. And the potential Universal Church ultimately needs them as much as they need the Church. Worse still, all those earnestly seeking union with God in other great faiths would be excluded. But these too are the potential members of the true Holy Catholic Church of the future. This book is therefore addressed to all who understand the cause of mankind's gathering difficulties, and are prepared for the supreme endeavour involved in finding the only way out. For there is only one true way out of suffering. This is the Way into Supreme Joy, God. Christ is the only Way, by whatever name He be known. And His Body is the Church, by whatever name it be called. It is not the sign that concerns us, but the thing that is signified.

A word of caution is necessary here, however. The present order of civilization is decaying. It is decaying inevitably, since it represents a phase of human history in which man has lost the Way into Reality, and is thus somnambulant. The circumstances under which this civilization's death may occur grow more horrifying each year. Those who grasp the ultimate purpose of human existence should be reconciled to the prospect of an agony which must sooner or later recall man to the Way into God. As they should be reconciled to the possible agony of their own death. But there may be others to whom these issues are not equally clear. Such may attempt the Way into God as a *means of saving* the present order of civilization and *of avoiding* the agony of its end. This book is not for them. For to them God is a means, not the End of all ends. To them God is a means of their personal earthly happiness. The Way into God would for them therefore become the way to destruction.

[3]

The second feature to be looked for in those to whom this book is addressed is a certain degree of intensity in their need for God, a certain degree of intensity in their interest in, their longing for God.

Every human need is satisfied in three main stages. They are closely related, yet distinguishable. First the mind comes into play; the need and the possibilities of satisfying it are known (cognized). Then the heart becomes involved; the feelings (affections) are aroused in the form of desires or aversions. Lastly the will is set in motion; the striving (conation) commences to satisfy the desires or aversions. These three stages are pre-eminently present in the case of the most fundamental of all human needs, the need for God.

Everyone who seriously sets out to seek God must begin by studying God. To be more precise, he begins by studying the recorded experience of those who have found God, in short the Holy Scriptures. He probably finds the Scriptures hard to understand. He turns to commentaries. These may lead him on to theology and possibly to philosophy. Some, or all, of this study is necessary to lead him on to the second stage in his search. This is the stage of the heart, in which he actually begins to desire God. But if study becomes an end in itself, the search breaks down. The mind of the seeker alone is involved. His heart remains untouched. He is without desire for God. He knows *about* God, but does not seek knowledge *of* God. The student never becomes the aspirant.

The approaches to the Way into God are littered with such impotents. The enormous proliferation of sterile theological speculation alone gives one some notion of the numbers of seekers who have become bogged down in studying the Way into God without actually entering upon it.

If comparatively few ever reach the stage of desiring union with God, even fewer reach the last stage of actually striving for it. This book is addressed to all those whose need for God has reached the degree at which they are not merely interested in the problem of union with God, but at which they actually desire this and are prepared to work for it. To work for this as the supreme purpose of human existence. For only here does the Way into God truly begin.

How is one to be sure of having reached this point? The answer is: when further study seems barren and useless. When books, such as were once opened with eager interest and expectancy as guides to the Truth, as revelations of the purpose of existence, now seem a string of empty words. When philosophical and theological speculations seem mere churning of water, capable of being kept up indefinitely without any useful results. When words and concepts themselves begin to seem mere sounds and empty symbols.

To imply that boredom with study is a sign of having outgrown the need for study may seem rather dangerous. It may even seem to contradict the previous insistence on the importance of sound doctrine, learning, tradition. The sign is trustworthy, however, only when the boredom springs from a desire, not merely to drop study, but to *pass beyond* study. The sign is trustworthy when, having studied God, the student wishes to prove from experience that God really is what He is proclaimed to be. The sign is most trustworthy of all when God begins to seem, not only interesting, intellectually satisfying, but desirable, *fascinating*; not only the solution of all problems, but the *mysterium tremendum et fascinans*.

Someone may perhaps remark on the absurdity of addressing a book to those who have outgrown the usefulness of books. The answer is that this book is intended to carry the student beyond books to experience, to change him into an active aspirant to union with God, and ultimately into a true disciple, in the fullest sense a *follower* of Jesus Christ, the Forerunner into God.

[4]

The third and last feature to be looked for in those to whom this book is addressed is an integrated view of God and man, and the relationship between them. The actual terms in which these views are expressed here need not of course be accepted in detail. But whoever rejects their essential sense will hardly find this book relevant.

One may ask how such an enormous subject can be compressed into a few pages without hopeless distortion. Only of course by summarizing its bare essence, and leaving out all technical detail. Some students of these matters may not much like the result. They will certainly find as many holes in it as they like. But then, like a net, a summary inevitably consists mostly of holes. The only criticism worthy of notice will be an alternative summary which is no less sound. Perhaps the reader might also profitably remember that the subject is not only the largest, but the most complicated one in existence.

Our summary opens with a view of God. It is of course impossible adequately to describe God, let alone 'sum Him up'. Yet the experience of God *has* been put into words. It is on these records, especially the Holy Scriptures, that our view is based. For God reveals Himself most directly through this experience. He is indeed present in it Himself.

We have already seen that God is the One Reality, Eternal, Perfect. Thus God is The All, as well as the Source of All. God is The One Who is above all, and through all, and in all.[1] We further saw that the One Reality is not impersonal, but personal. For the personal is above the impersonal. Man is personal. God must therefore be super-personal. But what does this really mean?

One may say that the essential characteristic of human personality is self-consciousness, in other words, man's awareness of himself as an I am. God must then be Super-conscious, All-conscious, aware of The ALL as I AM. Which is how God is actually described in one of the Bible's most profound passages. I AM THAT I AM.[2]

We now go into a little more detail. An I am is primarily a unity. But an I am is necessarily also a trinity. Or it would not be an I am. So, for instance, unless a thinker, his thinking and his thoughts *all* exist, *none* of them can exist. Unless I can know myself, I am not self-conscious, not truly an I am. The triune I am thus consists of subject, object and the mutual relations between

[1] Eph. 4. 6. [2] Exod. 3. 14.

these. In other words, of the I, the me, and all those processions between them which constitute the thinking, feeling and striving quality of an I am. One may say, in short, that I am, the unity, *manifests* as I am, the trinity.

We therefore begin by stating that I AM is first and foremost the Supreme Unity, the One Who is above all, and through all, and in all.[1] The Supreme One always remains utterly ineffable and beyond all that could ever be predicated of Him.[2] But since He is knowable—or the Scriptures would not exist—He must manifest Himself. He does so as the Three-in-One. His Trinity is His very first manifestation, the Triune Word expressed by the One. All further manifestation proceeds from the Word.[3]

The One is thus the Father, the Supreme Subject, the I. Being Love, He eternally expresses, or gives, Himself in Love. He thereby begets the Triune Son, the Supreme Object, the ME. The Son is the perfect image of the Father. Hence the Son also gives Himself in Love. He thereby not only remains one with the Father, but *makes* all things visible and invisible, The All. This, too, in all its multiplicity, gives itself in every conceivable form and degree of love. The All, through the Three, is thus gathered together again in One.[4] So the I, the ME and the mutual self-giving in Love constitute the Nature and Life of the Divine I AM. And in this supreme sense I AM is the All-conscious All, as well as the Source of All.

[5]

We now come to our summary of man. Because so much more *appears* to be known of man than of God, our summary may be rather more controversial. Theologians, and possibly philosophers, are alone likely to be our critics there. Here we shall also draw the fire of psychologists and possibly biologists, not to mention 'men of the world'.

Theologians, psychologists and biologists usually concentrate attention on their own particular aspects of man, paying little attention to any others. The picture that each produces of man is thus almost bound to be one-sided. So, for instance, the theologian regards man mainly as a spiritual being. The psychologist regards

[1] Eph. 4. 6.
[2] 1 Tim. 6. 16.
[3] John 1. 3.
[4] Eph. 1. 10.

him mainly as a string of thoughts, feelings and strivings. The biologist regards him as little more than a living bundle of bones, muscles and nerves. Small wonder, then, that the discussion of man's essential identity arouses as much heat as it does.

The attempt to combine the points of view of theologians, psychologists and biologists usually results in a description of man as being composed of body, soul and spirit. We accept this description as sound, in principle. But as all three terms in it are used in so many different senses and are therefore quite ambiguous, for most people, and as in any case no very clear picture of man as a *unity* emerges from them, we shall have not only to clarify them, but to integrate them into a whole.

The first thing we shall do is to get rid of the *static* picture of man which is created by the description of him as composed of body, soul and spirit. Instead we shall try to present him as a developing, or rather awakening being, individually as well as collectively. It will therefore be more correct to begin by saying that man *starts* his conscious existence on earth as a body. Or, more exactly, as a conscious physical organism. His first purpose in life is therefore that of any other physical organism. This is to develop to maturity, to maintain himself in his environment, and to reproduce himself.[1] The vitality in him, of which he represents a form, thus flows into three great motives, enabling him to fulfil himself. These are his three main driving forces. The first to come into play in him is the one which drives him on to develop to maturity, and thus to solve his first main life-problem. This is the motive of self-preservation. When he has to some degree done this, he is in a position to attempt the solution of the next problem. The second of his great motives then comes into play, the one which drives him on to maintain himself in his environment. This is self-assertion. When he has to some degree solved his second life-problem, he attempts the third and last. The third of his great motives now comes into play. This is the one which drives him on to reproduce himself, and thereby to fulfil himself as a physical organism. This is the motive of self-giving.

Most human beings fulfil themselves on this level, at any rate to some degree. Many of them exhaust their vitality in doing so,

[1] To use language borrowed from E. S. Russell's *Interpretation of Development and Heredity*.

and never develop further, never really become aware of a richer purpose in life. Their consciousness thus remains largely the product of their three great motives in interaction with their environment. One may say that their I am is mainly an intermittent series of feelings of two main kinds. One consists of the thoughts, emotions and strivings involved in the pursuit of self-fulfilment. The other consists of the pleasures and pains accompanying success or failure of the pursuit. They are conscious, of course, but not *properly* self-conscious. That is to say, they are not properly aware of their selves, their I am, as distinct from their bodies. They identify their selves with their bodies. 'I am my body,' they might say, if pressed to define their essential selves.

[6]

Let us leave man in this relatively primitive stage, and trace his further development. This is carried on by those human beings whose vitality is not exhausted by the struggle for self-fulfilment as bodies, and which thus enables them to reach out for richer self-fulfilment. The thoughts, emotions and strivings involved in the activity of the three great motives in them grow more intense and elaborate. So do the pleasures and pains accompanying success or failure in their pursuit of self-fulfilment. The intermittent series of feelings become united into a continuous chain, with the result that consciousness grows into self-consciousness. Becoming aware of the distinction between their body and their self, they become properly conscious of their I am, properly self-conscious. They now identify their selves, not with their bodies so much as with their thoughts, feelings and strivings. '*I am* my thoughts, feelings, and strivings,' they might say.

One may say that their soul, their *I am* is born in them. But the soul is prior to body. *I am* is prior to 'I am'. Or the lesser would have produced the greater. Which is philosophically absurd. Hence it is really more correct to say that *I am* awakes in them. So they become, not merely conscious bodies, merely nominally 'I am', but self-conscious, truly *I am*. And they begin to pursue self-fulfilment, not only as bodies, but as souls, as *I ams*. To fulfil themselves they must again mature, maintain themselves in their environment, and reproduce themselves. But since they are now conscious of themselves, they must do so, not only as conscious bodies, but as self-conscious *I ams*.

Self-conscious man is incomparably more thoughtful, emotional and conative than merely conscious man. The first stage in his pursuit of self-fulfilment on this higher level consists of his struggle to mature as an *I am*. He is mainly governed here again by the first of his three great motives, self-preservation. His *I am*, struggling to mature, thus mainly consists of feelings of dependence in many varieties. When he has to some degree solved the first life-problem, he attacks the second. This is to maintain his *I am* is his environment. Here he is mainly governed by the second of his great motives, self-assertion. His *I am* now mainly consists of feelings of egoism, again in every conceivable variety. He feels himself to be the centre of the universe and strives to *use* it as far as he can. He strives, in other words, to impose his personal will upon his environment, which he regards as existing solely for his benefit. When he has to some degree asserted himself, he attacks the third and last of his life-problems. This is to reproduce his *I am*. He begins to be governed by the third of his great motives, self-giving. His *I am* now consists mainly of other-regarding or altruistic feelings. He now strives, not to impose his will, but rather to propagate his views, ideas and values, not for his own benefit, but for that of others.

In the present dispensation self-conscious man fulfils himself far more rarely than merely conscious man. In the first place, because this is intrinsically far more difficult. In the second place, because self-conscious man is his own greatest enemy. Being a relatively recent phenomenon in the process of human awakening, his *I am* is still poorly organized and integrated. Hence the welter of thoughts, emotions and strivings composing his *I am* is constantly liable to conflict. The very fact that he has risen above the merely bodily level exposes him to conflict. For his striving for self-fulfilment on the lower level is constantly liable to reawaken and clash with his striving on the higher level. Sexual desire, for instance, is liable to clash with altruism.

He may understand that self-fulfilment on the lower level must be sacrificed to self-fulfilment on the higher, if he is to fulfil himself more richly. But his will is by no means always able to enforce the sacrifice. His self-consciousness, his *I am*, is thus always liable to disintegration from within.

The third reason why self-conscious man finds it so difficult to fulfil himself is that he is almost as great an enemy of his neighbour as he is of himself. The more single-mindedly any *I am* strives to *use* the world, the more certain is the clash with every other *I am* also striving to *use* the world. The better self-conscious man thus survives his own *I am's* disintegration, the more liable he is to disintegrate his neighbour's *I am*.

In the present dispensation, therefore, man is the greatest cause of human suffering. The welter of self-conscious individuals, themselves a welter of conflicting feelings, each struggling to impose his will upon the other, combining and re-combining in temporary coalitions great and small, as these happen to serve his predatory interests for the moment, constantly frustrate each other's self-fulfilment, and thus cause each other suffering. Being far more sensitive than merely conscious man, his suffering is that much more intense. In sum, self-conscious man not only finds happiness much more rarely than conscious man, but his suffering is much more intense.

[7]

Let us leave man in this critical stage of development, into which the *masses* of Western society are entering in increasing numbers in the mid-twentieth century, the stage in which the happiness of unself-conscious self-fulfilment on the bodily level has been left behind and the next stage not yet attained, and trace his further development. In the present dispensation a small advance guard only reaches this higher level. Those few self-conscious individuals, who are either especially gifted or who enjoy a particularly favourable environment, manage to fulfil themselves as *I ams*, and thus become capable of still richer self-fulfilment. As always, they become dissatisfied with their attainment. In this case, with the successful propagation of their thoughts, feelings and strivings and the ideas, values and views springing from these. They become bored, perhaps, with the whole state of self-consciousness. Their *I am*, indeed, may altogether become a burden to them, if only implicitly.

Let us suppose that in such a situation they meet the message of the Gospel in terms that appeal to them. In terms, in other words, that they really understand. The Message is similar in all the great faiths, though clearest in Christianity, at any rate for Western man.

'Come unto me, all ye that labour and are heavy laden, and I will give you rest.'[1]

'If any man would come after me, let him deny himself, and take up his cross, and follow me.'[2]

'Where I am, there shall also my servant be.'[3]

'Abide in me, and I in you.'[4]

Let us further suppose that they recognize here the promise, both of deliverance from the boredom and burden of self-consciousness, and also of the ultimate satisfaction of their search for *supreme* self-fulfilment. Let us suppose that they are clearly and soundly instructed in the sovereign science and art of inheriting these great and precious promises. And let us finally suppose that they actually enter upon the supreme adventure of denying the self, of crucifying the *I am*, and of resting or abiding in Christ. Then, as they steadfastly persevere, the string of thoughts, feelings and strivings, and the ideas, values and views that arise from them and compose their *I am*, begin to die. As they steadfastly, earnestly and single-mindedly seek Christ, they gradually come to be 'where I AM'.

So they are spiritually reborn. Their spiritual life truly begins. Christ is said to be born in them. But here again the impression may be that the greater has evolved from the lesser. Which would be philosophically more absurd than ever. For Christ is the Eternal Word, the Eternal Manifestation of the Supreme Unmanifested One Who is above all, and through all, and in all. The lesser is therefore as nothing before the Supreme. Hence it is clearer to say that Christ is revealed in their soul.[5] Self-consciousness in them gives way to, or rather surrenders to, All-consciousness. I AM becomes incarnate, becomes flesh in them, so that, ceasing to be *I ams*, they begin to be I AM. They come to know their *true* selves to be, not *I am*, but I AM. They begin to 'be made perfect in One'.[6]

[1] Matt. 11. 28. [2] Mark 8. 34 R.V. [3] John 12. 26.
[4] John 15. 4. [5] Rom. 8. 18. [6] John 17. 23.

[8]

It remains for us to sketch our view of the relationship between God and man. A good deal of this has already been implied in the last few sections, of course, and all we need is to bring out the main outline. Even this may be unnecessary for an imaginative reader. But since we are following the Bible as closely as possible, it is necessary to show that our view is not a mere bit of inductive or deductive reasoning, but purely Biblical. Some may find it a little startling at first. The Biblical authority for it could, however, hardly be clearer.

One of the marks of all the great religions is a more or less explicit affirmation of man's Divine origin. This is nowhere clearer than in the Bible. Man is in so many words stated to have been made in the image or likeness of God.[1] But man fell from that status. The Bible is equally clear on that point. From here, however, space forces us to compress the Bible very severely. We may say that man's fall from his original status was so great that the memory of this status was all but obliterated in him. But not quite. The clearest trace left behind by that vestigial memory was the more or less vague hope of redemption from the Fall. It would be fascinating to trace the gradual crystallization of that hope into a vision of that event. It is surely the very essence of man's developing awareness, of his spiritual awakening, and perfectly expresses the unfolding of religion up to the Incarnation. But we have no space for this. All we can say here is that this hope was fulfilled in Jesus Christ. More completely, indeed, than any but a very exceptional few had suspected possible. They alone realized the hope's fulfilment, as well as the fullness of that fulfilment. And it is still not generally realized. Let *us*, at any rate, try to grasp its meaning as clearly, explicitly and as deeply as we can. Nothing could declare it more plainly than the Bible does, and we revert to it in detail once more.

The Old Testament declares man to have been made in the image of God, but to have fallen from that status. The New Testament declares Jesus Christ to be the Image of God.[2] Jesus Christ was unique, not only in the sense that any person-

[1] Gen. I. 26, 27.   [2] Heb. I. 3 R.V.

ality is unique, but because He was the *full* Manifestation or Word in space and time of the One Who is above all, and through all, and in all. Unique though He is, however, the New Testament declares Him to be the Forerunner, the First-born of many brethren, and the First-fruits of them that slept.[1] We have already stated the purpose of the Incarnation.[2] God, in the words of Athanasius, was made man, that we might be made God. We can now restate this in terms of man's relationship with God. In Jesus Christ man was wholly redeemed from his fall, resuming his eternal status as the Image of God, the Manifestation of the One. Union with God is therefore more correctly described as Re-union. Which is precisely how the Bible does describe it. 'God was in Christ, reconciling the world unto himself.'[3]

It seems hard to pick a fair quarrel with this statement of the ultimate relationship between God and man. But its very orthodoxy, and possibly familiarity, are liable to obscure the depth of its meaning, especially its practical meaning. What does this really mean in terms of experience, at any rate in the mid-twentieth century? We have now therefore to translate the familiar conventional statement into the language we have been using in the last few sections. This language is no invention of our own. As we have seen, it is fully Biblical where God is concerned. Where man is concerned, it needs no justifying. And if it is not usual to speak of man as an unfolding or awakening *I am*, it is only because we are slaves of the naïve human habit of objectifying, of making *things* of all we know, including the knowing subject. But man is not primarily an object. He is primarily a knowing subject. With this in mind, let us then proceed with our translation.

God is The One Who is not only The All, but the Source of All. The One is I AM. I AM is necessarily triune, consisting of the Supreme I, the Subject, the Source; of the Supreme ME, the Object, the All; and of the mutual self-giving in Love which constitutes the All-creating, All-sustaining and All-perfecting activity of I AM. The I loves, and thus begets the ME, and through the ME makes the ALL. The ALL reflects or returns this Love, and thereby through the ME returns into the I. We may therefore try to conceive I AM as the eternally abiding One, eternally proceeding

[1] Heb. 6. 20; Rom. 8. 29; 1 Cor. 15. 20.
[2] Section 1 in the Introduction.
[3] 2 Cor. 5. 19.

into (and so making) the All, and from the All eternally returning into (and so being gathered together) the One. Which is precisely what I AM declares Himself to be. 'I AM Alpha and Omega, the beginning and the ending.'[1]

Now it is quite clear that at some point in the procession of The One-in-Three into the multiplicity of The All a 'splitting' into 'fragments' must take place. Or The One would not become The Many of which The All also consists. Here is where the Fall must have occurred. An abuse of freedom, necessarily possessed by the Image of God, must have taken place. Man, as it were, broke out of the Divine Procession and fell into independent separateness. Man fell out of Unity. So the Image of The Three-in-One was shattered in him. Or one may say that he ceased to be his true self as the ME of the Divine I AM. Rather perhaps as a man ceases to be his true, fully aware self in sleep.

But I AM did not cease to love the fallen fragment of His Image, of His ME. For I AM is Love. That Love at once began to draw man back to the Source of his being, to his true state as the ME of the Divine I AM. At first he heard the Call but faintly. The Prophets', Sages', Seers' hopes of redemption represent the extent of man's awareness in those early stages. But driven on by suffering, realizing that the fleshpots were filled with swine's husks, he began to seek his home in his Father's Mansion. This was his *true* self, I AM, though as yet he was very far from knowing it.

As he sought, inevitably he found.[2] Having become conscious of his self as a body, driven on by further suffering, he became self-conscious, conscious of his self as *I am*. Here his suffering immensely increased. Finally he was able to hear the Call in its supreme fullness. And so man entered upon All-consciousness, and became perfectly aware of his self as the ME of the Divine I AM. That is to say, he fully awoke to his *true* identity, to his *true* self, and knew himself to be the ME of the Divine I AM.

From this summit, this hyparxis of The All, He called upon His brethren to awake from sleep, to arise from the dead, and to abide in Him.[3] Whoever follows Him, accepting all that this im-

[1] Rev. 1. 8; 21. 6; 22. 13. Capitals used to emphasize the meaning.
[2] Matt. 7. 7; Luke 11. 9.
[3] Speaking through His Apostle Paul and through His own Incarnate Self.

plies, through Him regains his eternal status as the ME of the Divine I AM.

Now he who is able to do so, acknowledging the Son, 'hath the Father also'.[1] He 'hath both the Father and the Son'.[2] He has I AM. He knows his true self to be I AM. He knows The One Who is above all, and through all, and in all, to be his own true self.

Hitherto we have seen man's awakening as reunion with God, as his return into God. We have thus seen the tremendous process from below, from the human point of view. And rightly so, for to complete the process is the supreme purpose of human existence. Not only in this world, but in any other we may have to pass through on our way into God. But in order to prevent any possibility of fancying *ourselves climbing* into God, it is also necessary to glance at the process from above, from the Divine point of view, in so far as one can say so. This is the supreme, complete, all-comprehending view. From here man's ascent is seen *also* to be God's descent.[3] Man's realization of his true self is seen to be God's gift of Himself to man, so that God, the Supreme SELF, may be all in all.[4]

'When God gave Himself *for* me, He gave Himself *to* me; and when God gave Himself *to* me, He gave me back my own *true* self.'

Whoever proves the truth of these words *to the uttermost*, returns into God. In him the relationship between God and man, I AM and *I am*, comes to an end. His self, having died, is made perfect in One.[5] He has inherited God.[6] He has become the First and the Last, Whose Descent and Ascent are the Heartbeat, the Beginning and the Ending of the All.[7]

[1] 1 John 2. 23.
[2] 2 John 9.
[3] John 3. 13; Eph. 4. 9, 10.
[4] 1 Cor. 15. 28.
[5] John 17. 23.
[6] Rom. 8. 17; Gal. 4. 7.
[7] Rev. 1. 8. Whether he enters upon his inheritance here or hereafter is irrelevant at present.

Chapter Two

The Anatomy of Belief

[1]

WE HAVE SEEN that the purpose of the Incarnation was to bring man back into God. We have also seen that the chief means of bringing about this saving Reunion are the two great Sacraments. Or, to use the language we have adopted here for the sake of clarity, the two great Sacraments are the chief means of bringing about the transformation of the fallen, human, self-conscious *I am* into the All-conscious Divine I AM. For that is what Reunion with God means in practice. And that alone is what constitutes Salvation. No wonder, then, that God Incarnate Himself instituted the two great Sacraments.

As nothing in life could be as important as this for any human being, we need not be afraid of labouring the point in reminding ourselves of the tremendous significance of the Sacraments. In Holy Baptism man is incorporated into God, through Christ. By this means we are enabled to respond to Christ's call to abide in Him.[1] The Holy Communion is the means of taking into ourselves Christ's Body and Blood. This is, of course, directly based upon His declaration that whosoever eats His flesh and drinks His blood dwells in Him and He in him.[2] According to Hebrew symbolism the body or flesh of a creature signified its nature or essential being, while its blood signified its life. The Holy Communion is therefore the means of taking into ourselves the Divine Nature and Life. And here Christ's promise to abide in those who abide in Him is fulfilled. So the two great Sacraments represent the means of Reunion with God in a visible and tangible form which the blindest and crudest materialist cannot, with fairness, fail to appreciate.

In setting out upon the Way of Reunion with God, therefore, we realize clearly that all we shall try to think, feel and do must be based, four-square, upon the two Sacraments. We shall find it

[1] John 15. 4. [2] John 6. 56.

increasingly helpful to remember this as we ascend and the Way grows ever harder. When some aspiration appears fantastically beyond human attainment, when even the language in which it is expressed seems blasphemous, not to say nonsensical, these visible and tangible signs will sustain us. We shall see in them a guarantee, a very pledge of the truth and actuality of the Divine Promise. Above all, they will keep us from straying into fanciful aberrations of thought and feeling and action. They will keep us firmly tied to the soberly practical business of following in the wake of our supreme Forerunner.[1]

We shall do well, then, to begin by reviewing one or two salient features of the two great Rites so that their familiar words may come to life for us; so that their soberly practical meaning may come home to us; so that we may know exactly, in fact, just what and how we shall have to think, feel and act if our *I am* is to become transformed into the Divine I AM.

[2]

The Rite of Holy Baptism may be said to open with a somewhat detailed prayer for the Grace of the Sacrament. 'O merciful God, grant that the old Adam in this person may be so *buried*, that the new man may be *raised* up in him . . . that all carnal affections may *die* in him, and that all things belonging to the Spirit may *live* and *grow* in him.' The Sacrament is then administered. Immediately afterwards thanks are given for the Grace bestowed. 'We yield thee hearty thanks, most merciful Father, that it has pleased thee to *regenerate* this person with thy Holy Spirit, and to *receive* him for thine own child by adoption into thy Holy Church.' The Rite ends with a prayer for the *completion* of the process begun in Holy Baptism. 'Grant, O Lord, that being *buried* with Christ by baptism into his death, he may also be made partaker of his *resurrection*.'[2]

Now for the rendering of these prayers into the language we are using in this book. To paraphrase them might beg various questions, and possibly obscure rather than clarify their essential meaning. This is best conveyed by a rather free translation.

The celebrant begins by praying that the person's old, fallen,

[1] Matt. 8. 22; 9. 9; 16. 24; 19. 21; John 10. 27; 12. 26, etc.

[2] The 1928 Prayer Book is quoted here, though the italics are mine in order to emphasize the salient features of the Baptismal Service.

human, self-conscious *I am* may be so destroyed that the new, risen, All-conscious Divine I AM may be born in him . . . that human feelings may die in him, and that all the attributes of the Spirit may come to life and grow in him. Having administered the Sacrament, the celebrant gives thanks for the regeneration of the *I am* by the Spirit of I AM, and for its adoption as the ME of I AM by incorporation into the Body of that ME. The celebrant ends by praying that the person's *I am*, having been buried, may rise and grow up as the Divine I AM.

We now turn to the second of the two great Sacraments. The salient features of the Holy Communion are even more clearly and sharply marked. They are, in fact, wholly contained in the last sentence of what must be one of the most tremendous prayers in existence, the Prayer of Humble Access. 'Grant us, gracious Lord, *so* to eat the flesh of thy dear Son Jesus Christ, and to drink his blood, that our sinful bodies may be made clean by his body, and our souls washed through his most precious blood, and that we may evermore dwell in him, and he in us.'

The translation of this prayer into our language is quickly made. In the Prayer of Humble Access the celebrant plainly asks that the communicants may *so* partake of the Divine Nature and Life that their own *I ams* may be purged of all their carnal and emotional entanglements, and that in consequence they may eternally abide in the Divine I AM, and I AM in them.

The two great Sacraments are thus seen to be a two-sided (subjective-objective) means of undergoing the most radical and fundamental of all conceivable changes, the transformation of the human into the Divine. It is not extravagant to call this transformation the transfiguration. The vision on the Mount of Transfiguration may well have been a glimpse of a process which was completed by our Forerunner, and which mankind is now struggling to complete in His wake. Be that as it may, the essence of the process is the purgation to the uttermost, indeed the crucifixion of the old, fallen, human, self-conscious *I am* and its rebirth, resurrection and ascension as the Divine I AM. May we not regard the Birth, Ministry, Crucifixion, Resurrection and Ascension of Jesus Christ as a more detailed and explicit, a more exoteric version of the Transfiguration suited to mankind's myopia?

[3]

We now possess some notion of *what* the Sacraments empower man to receive and to undergo. We must next see *how* this comes about. We must see, in fact, what our part in the tremendous process amounts to. For the Grace of the Sacraments is not thrust upon us in some automatic, mechanical or magical manner, such as operates in fairy-tales or dreams. The Grace has to be received. Rather as the eyes have to be opened if the light of the sun is to be seen.

The conventional answer to our question is, of course, simple. The Grace of the Sacraments is received by faith. We receive power to undergo the transformation according to our faith. But here again we must ask what this really means in practice. And the more familiar we are with the (perfectly correct) answer, the more necessary this probably is.

Let us begin by studying carefully the very brief but very exact and practical instructions which our Forerunner has laid down on *how* to ask. For He speaks with the supreme authority of One Who has actually accomplished the transformation in full, and Who is therefore God. He does not, of course, refer specifically to the Sacraments. He goes to the root of the matter, and lays down the only way in which man, embedded in the temporal order, can receive *any* gift from the Eternal Order, Grace in any form.

'Have faith in God. Verily I say unto you, whosoever shall say unto this mountain, be thou taken up and cast into the sea; and shall not doubt in his heart, but shall believe that what he saith cometh to pass; he shall have it. Therefore I say unto you, all things whatsoever ye pray and ask for, believe that ye have received them, and ye shall have them.'[1]

Let us now carefully consider these laconic but extremely pregnant instructions upon which so much depends. We begin by noting the part played by feeling and experience in all belief, and particularly in all prayerful asking. We remind ourselves that the human personality consists of thinking, feeling and striving, or mind, heart and will. For the present we leave out the third great

[1] Mark 11. 24 R.V.

side of the personality, the will. We begin therefore by noting that it is the heart, the whole feeling or experiencing side of ourselves which, in the first place, determines the depth of our faith. A little reflection will soon bear this out. If we consider the psychology of belief, we may say that belief begins when we accept some proposition with the mind. But it is quite obvious that the heart need not be involved in this in the least, so that the belief may extend no deeper than mere mental assent to a proposition. For instance, we may mentally accept the fact that, God being Almighty as well as All-loving, nothing essentially harmful can ever befall us. None the less we may *fear* a whole variety of real or imaginary dangers, and thereby clearly prove that we have by no means accepted that fact with the feelings, with the heart. Again, we may pray for some Divine gift, and be thoroughly convinced mentally that God will not fail in His promise to give us what we ask, as the Lord explicitly tells us.[1] Yet we may not in the least be convinced of this in our heart of hearts, to use a very apt colloquialism. We may easily go on *feeling* quite unconvinced. We may continue to doubt in our heart, in fact, as the Lord so graphically puts it in the passage just quoted.[2] All of which makes it clear that belief of this kind is certainly not deep enough to enable us to receive whatever we ask for in prayer.

Having admitted this fatal defect, the very practical question of overcoming it now arises. How are we to cease to doubt in our hearts? Is there any way in which we may become convinced, in which we may come to believe with the heart as well as with the mind? How is our faith in God to involve, not merely the mind, but the whole feeling or experiencing side of our personality? For without this our faith remains superficial, not deep enough to enable us to receive more than nominally whatever we ask for.

As always, the Lord's instructions contain the complete answer to our question. His instructions may sometimes seem cryptic and difficult to grasp, but paradoxically this is because they are so utterly clear, direct and exact. They thus pass through the naturally woolly human mind as a sharp needle through fatty flesh, leaving little trace. This was so always in the last two thousand years. It is particularly so in the mid-twentieth century, when even the average mind considered adequately educated is so much

[1] Luke 11. 13. [2] Mark 11. 24 R.V.

more disorganized and disintegrated than hitherto, and therefore more sluggish in response to the tremendous news of the Gospel. As we are all in this unhappy position, simply by virtue of being embedded in the present century, it will greatly help us to recognize the situation. We need note no more than its barest essentials. A little self-analysis will do the rest.

The invention of printing has made possible an enormous proliferation of literature on every subject, particularly during the present century. We are all thus exposed to a deluge of words conveying ideas of all kinds. It would be impossible to digest them all without loss of sanity. Most of them are unworthy of being absorbed anyway. We thus unconsciously become insensitive to the printed or spoken word. The nett result is that our minds are not only apt to become a jumble of superficial and mutually unrelated ideas, but barriers against deep experience. Not only are we thus badly equipped to grasp the needle-sharp understatements of the Gospel, but we are sluggish in digesting them. Even when our minds accept them, our hearts are all too apt to remain unaffected.

Let us then return to the Lord's instructions, where the complete answer to our question lies, and try to grasp their needle-sharp point. The sentence we have already studied *suggests* the answer. 'Whosoever . . . shall not doubt in his heart, but shall believe that what he saith *cometh* to pass. . . .' Not *will* come to pass, or *shall* come to pass, let it be noted; but *cometh* to pass. That is to say *now*, at the time of saying or asking or praying. And when we turn to the last sentence of the Lord's instructions, we find the answer we are looking for, complete and explicit. 'All things whatsoever ye pray and ask for, believe that ye *have* received them, and ye shall have them.'[1]

Now let us carefully study these words. We should be on our guard against allowing their significance to elude us by their very simplicity. We begin by considering how we normally believe that we have received any object we ask for in the world. Suppose we ask for a pound note. A piece of paper is handed to us. We assure ourselves, with a glance or with a more careful examination, that the piece of paper we have been handed really is a pound note. And only then do we receive it *as such*. In other words, we

[1] Mark 11. 24 R.V. (My italics.)

have the pound note only when we believe that we actually have received it, only after we have actually felt or experienced a pound note as having come into our possession. This is precisely what the Lord tells us to do when asking in prayer.

The less tangible, the more spiritual the gift we ask for, the more obviously necessary this is. If we ask for peace, for instance, how can we possibly receive peace unless we first feel peaceful, and thus believe that we *have* received peace? We *must* believe that we have received it before we can have it. Or we cannot *possibly* receive it. For to feel it in us, and thus to believe that we have received it, is the only *possible* way of receiving it.

The answer to our question is therefore as follows. It is only through training that we cease to feel doubtful, that our heart becomes convinced, that we come to have faith and to believe, not with the mind alone, but also with the heart. Or more exactly, our heart needs training, so that we may come to experience or feel the Grace of the Sacrament pouring into us, and therefore to believe that we *have* received that Grace. Only so shall we, and can we, receive that Grace. This fact must be faced, whatever the danger may be of such emphasis on experience or feeling.

[4]

We have now begun to come down to the practical details without which spiritual directions remain mere platitudes, and without which the spiritual life itself remains a pious hope rather than actual communion with God, not to mention the actual return into God. But we have not come down to details far enough yet. One or two questions still remain to be dealt with.

The first may only occur to a few readers and may seem theoretical rather than practical. Most readers will probably have been baptized half a lifetime or more ago. To begin trying to receive the Grace of the Sacrament, the power to destroy the *I am* in order to be raised as I AM, so many years after it was conferred may strike them as somewhat unrealistic.

The answer surely is that Grace is not turned on, as it were, with the administration of the Sacrament, and off again with the completion of the rite. Any such view would imply that Grace is *wrung* from God in the Sacrament, and suggests magic rather than religion. The Sacrament, after all, merely manifests, at a given time and place, the Providential Grace which eternally proceeds from God as light pours from the sun. (There is also a return of Grace to God, of course, lifting the *I am* into I AM, but we are not at the moment concerned with this.) The Sacrament may thus be likened to a burning glass which concentrates the light and heat of the sun in order to enable an insensitive skin to become aware of this. The very existence of the Sacraments is really a measure of the human difficulty of receiving Grace. Which is no doubt the prime reason for the Lord's institution of them. As man, no less than God, He must have been perfectly aware of our human needs and weaknesses. Hence, though a few minutes may be spent in the administration of the Sacrament, its Grace may not begin to be *received* until much later. This must be so, indeed, in the case of infants. A whole lifetime may be spent in even making a start in receiving. As the Lord explicitly lays down, it is only as we believe that we *have* received that we actually *do* receive. And as we have seen, it is only so that we *can* receive in any intelligible sense.

We now come to the second question that is likely to be asked. Being more practical, and so for our purposes more important, it is likely to be asked by more readers than the first one. We have prayed, or others have prayed for us, that we may be incorporated in Christ. We have prayed that we may partake of the Divine Nature and Life. We have prayed, in short, that we may dwell in Christ, and He in us. And we have received the Sacraments which not only guarantee that our prayers are answered, but constitute the actual answer itself in a plainly tangible and visible form. We are therefore face to face with the effort of bringing ourselves to believe that we have received what we have asked for. We are face to face, to be exact, with the supreme endeavour of knowing, and therefore believing, ourselves *to be* dwelling in Christ, and He in us.

One who has never seriously tried to put the Lord's instructions into actual practice, may find all this detail rather tedious. He may consider that it labours the obvious and makes heavy weather of a simple matter. Having received the Sacraments, he may say, he is in Christ, and Christ is in him, and no more need be said.

But is that so *really*? Is he really in Christ? And is Christ really in him? Or is it all merely a matter of words? If he has really been in Christ, and He in him, he should be able to give at least some description of the experience. Can he suggest, however haltingly, what it *feels like* to be in the One Who is the First and the Last, the Almighty? Or, if this is asking too much of his powers of expression, can he describe the beginning of the transformation of his human self-conscious *I am* into the All-conscious Divine I AM? Can he portray the actual experience of even the first stage of that transformation, that is, the death of his *I am*? For without this no resurrection as I AM can even begin. A few such simple and obvious questions will soon reveal whether his notion of himself in Christ and Christ in him involves his heart, or whether his mind alone possesses the knowledge. Whether it is all a matter of words, symbols, metaphors to him. Or whether it is a matter of experienced fact.

He may reply that he does not expect to experience and feel himself in Christ, and Christ in him as yet, if at all in this life. He may say that whoever faithfully receives the Sacraments dwells in Christ, and Christ in him. The Sacraments are a guarantee of this, and any effort to make this seem more real to himself merely implies doubt, indeed lack of faith. He will fully know himself to be in Christ, and Christ in him, in God's good time, if only in the life to come.

But the Lord has said as clearly as anything can be said that we receive whatever we ask for only as we believe that we *have* received it. And we have seen that we cannot truly believe that we have received *anything* without at least some experience of it. Therefore the ineluctable conclusion is that our incorporation into Christ, and His dwelling in ourselves, does not even begin until we possess at least some experience of this. It is our experience, in fact, which constitutes the beginning of our presence in Him, and His in us. The Bible leaves us no excuse whatever for waiting for 'God's good time'. For God never ceases to call all men to be reconciled or reunited with himself. God is Love, and wills all men to be saved.[1] There is no salvation apart from union with Him. 'God's good time' is therefore *now*. 'Behold, now is the accepted time; behold, now is the day of salvation.'[2] As for

[1] 1 Tim. 2. 4. [2] 2 Cor. 6. 2.

relegating salvation to the 'life to come', this represents even greater confusion. 'The life to come' begins precisely at the moment of spiritual rebirth, that is, at the moment in which we truly begin to dwell in Christ, and He in us. At the moment, that is, in which we first know ourselves in Him and Him in us, not only with the mind, but with the heart, in experience.

At about this stage our answers are likely to call forth a rather strong protest. All this insistence upon experience, it may be said, simply reduces the Grace of the Sacraments to feeling, to a subjective state, and utterly ignores its objective reality. It very plainly implies that Grace becomes real only after we have induced ourselves to imagine it to be so. Such a view ultimately runs us into the danger of reducing God Himself into a product of the imagination.

It is not easy to deal with such a protest. Not because it is theologically, or even logically weighty, but because it is probably due to a conscious, or more likely unconscious shrinking from experience. From a shrinking, in fact, from the suffering and endeavour involved in the crucifixion and resurrection which constitute the transformation of *I am* into I AM. And the more violently the protest is made, the deeper its emotional roots are likely to lie. For this reason alone, not to mention lack of space, it is not worth trying to deal with the objection in over-much detail. No argument, however cogent, could certainly touch the subconscious roots of the protest. But dealt with it nevertheless must be. For it springs from a confusion which modern psychology has worse confounded.

We begin by agreeing that Grace is most certainly really, truly and objectively given in the Sacraments, whether it is known, experienced, felt, or not. We *must* agree, or contradict what we have already said. This is that the Sacraments merely focus, in the spatio-temporal order, the Divine Nature and Life which eternally proceeds or descends from God, making and sustaining all things, as light and heat proceed from the sun. We can now go further. We must realize that, if Grace were not really and objectively given, man could not even imagine himself receiving it. How could he? It would be utterly beyond his power. Rather as it would be utterly beyond a dog's power to imagine some human action it had never seen performed. Man simply *cannot* imagine any gift of God which is not included in the Unsearchable Riches of Christ substanding the Grace of the Sacraments. Whoever believes this to be possible, indeed, has himself reduced God to a product of the human imagination, in any case to a status inferior to man.

It is, of course, only too possible to imagine oneself to have received Grace, when one in fact has not *been able* to receive anything. But this is beside the point here, though such a possibility is probably one good reason for disliking the emphasis on the need for genuine experience in the spiritual life. We are not concerned here with self-deception, however. As we shall see later, whether we have received Grace, or only imagined this, is easily decided by the presence of the fruits of the Spirit in us, or not. But because there are dangers in the spiritual life, and far greater ones than mere self-deception, that is hardly a sound reason for refusing to pursue the ultimate purpose of human existence.

We therefore clearly recognize that, though Grace pours from God in boundless prodigality as the very Procession of His Divine Nature and Life, which is the ultimate Reality, it is by no means necessarily received. Any more than we see the sun's light when our eyes are closed. Grace is truly received only when it becomes real for us, only to the extent that it is really known or recognized as such. We begin by knowing this 'theoretically', with the mind. But until we know it 'practically', with the heart, (and, we shall see later, with the will), the knowledge is superficial, incomplete and rudimentary. And our reception of Grace is superficial, incomplete and rudimentary. Only partially real, that is to say. Could anything be more obvious? We are actually happy, after all, only to the extent that we know it, not only with the mind, but with the heart, that is to say, actually *feel* happy.

All this applies *a fortiori* to the communicant's dwelling in Christ, and Christ in him. Through the Sacrament he *really* dwells in Christ, and Christ in him. Most certainly. Where else could man dwell, but in the One Who is above all, and through all, and in all. Who else could fill him but the First and the Last? The Sacrament thus merely drives the Reality home to dormant, ignorant, insensitive man. But the Reality becomes real for any particular man only in so far as he knows it. And knows it, not only with the mind, but with the heart and, as we shall see later, with the will.

Some may still remain unconvinced. In that case it is impossible to say anything more. Except perhaps to repeat once more the Lord's words on the subject. 'All things whatsoever ye pray and ask for, believe that ye have received them, and ye shall have them.' We receive Grace only to the extent that we believe that we *have* received it. And we can believe this only to the extent that we know it with mind, heart and will, in short with the whole of our personality. Those who need no further convincing may feel wearied with the many variations on the single theme. If so, let them once more remember how enormously much depends upon the laboured point, and admit that we cannot ever really know the Way into God too well.

[5]

We now come down to the last and most practical question of all. We saw that, having asked to dwell in Christ, and for Him to dwell in us, we only do so in the degree that we begin to experience and feel this. How do we start to do so? We saw that training is necessary in order to grow in capacity to believe. How is that training to start? The experience of real dwelling in Christ and of being indwelt by Him is so utterly beyond normal human experience that even a beginning seems hopeless. A dog may express itself in barks, but this has no common ground whatever with human language. And the difference between dog and man is as nothing to the difference between natural man and God. How are we ever even to *begin* feeling what it is like to dwell in, and to be indwelt by, the First and the Last, the Almighty, the One Who is above all, and through all, and in all? The moment we begin to try to imagine this, our very imagination wilts and escapes into poetical notions or metaphysical abstractions. But however useful poetry or metaphysics may be in awakening us to the *possibility* of Life in Christ, they will not help us to draw the first breath of actual Life in Him. They may rouse our aspiration to be transformed into the glory of I AM. They cannot help us to *enter* upon the transformation. Any more than an aspiration to ascend Mount Everest would take us a single step up its slope. The more distinctly we try to feel ourselves in I AM, and I AM in ourselves, in fact, the less distinct, the more dim and abstract our notion of I

AM grows. Just as the longer we gaze at the sun, the source of mundane light, the less we see because we are blinded.

One obvious way out of the difficulty at once suggests itself. It is quite commonly used. I AM was incarnate in Jesus Christ. One of the main purposes of the Incarnation was to demonstrate the Way into God. It has been held, therefore, that if we would know I AM and 'what He is like', we have only to study the life, teaching and ministry of Jesus and to imitate Him as faithfully as possible. And so His words, actions and, possibly, appearance are imitated.

The attempt to know I AM by these means cannot take us beyond a certain point, at any rate in the present age. The reason for this, very briefly, is that Jesus was the incarnation of I AM, that is to say the effect of a cause. The Perfect Effect of the Supreme Cause. And it is impossible to achieve any effect except, so to say, through its proper cause. As impossible, for instance, as to exert power without being powerful. The opposite would be a trick or an illusion, and not a reality. The only effective way of trying to imitate Jesus, therefore, is to attempt to dwell in Christ, so that Christ may dwell in us, as in Jesus.

This error may lead to nothing worse than failure to dwell in Christ. But it may have worse results. It may substitute a merely ethical for a complete Christianity and therefore produce a travesty. Worst of all, it may lead to the idolatrous worship of an historical figure, as is proved by the periodical condemnations of 'Jesuolatry'. Whatever else the error leads to, however, it effectively prevents true union with God through Christ. The imitation of Jesus blocks the imitation of Christ.

How are we to take the first crucial step in knowing what Christ 'is like'? We must somehow imitate Jesus Christ, not superficially, as an ape might mimic a man, but *throughly*.[1] But how? A saying of His already quoted suggests an answer. When He spoke of Himself as the Way, He also spoke of Himself as the Truth and the Life.[2] This forcibly reminds us of the basic fact that Jesus Christ is as much God as man, and that the fullness of the Godhead dwells in Him bodily, in S. Paul's words.[3] What we must imitate, therefore, are not the words and actions of Jesus Christ the man, but the Nature and Life of Jesus Christ the Word of

[1] Ps. 51. 2. [2] John 14. 6. [3] Col. 2. 9.

God. We must not be afraid to attempt what S. Paul explicitly tells us to do, which is to imitate God Himself. 'Be ye therefore imitators of God.'[1]

Could anything ultimately be more obvious? How else is the human *I am* to be transformed into the Divine I AM? How else is Christ to dwell in us?

At first sight this seems to take us no further forward. The fullness of the sun's light still seems to blind us. How are we ever even to *begin* to imitate God? What is the Divine Nature and Life really *like*? What does it really *feel like* to be Divine?

Jesus Christ shows us the way every time He speaks, especially when He speaks as God. On all such occasions He directly reveals some facet of the Divine Nature and Life. He does so, for instance, when giving His Peace to His disciples.[2] He obviously speaks here as Christ, as God, as I AM. For a man cannot in any normal sense give 'his peace' to another. He further speaks of His Joy.[3] He speaks of His Love.[4] As we have already seen, He speaks of Himself as the Truth and the Life. He similarly reveals many other facets or attributes of I AM. Each of these is thus an aspect of the Divine Nature and Life. If we try to experience and feel each of these facets of I AM in ourselves, therefore, we shall clearly begin to feel at least something of what 'it is like' to dwell in Christ and to be indwelt by Him.

Some of these facets are clearly nearer to human experience than others. However far removed the peace of the world may be from Divine Peace, it is clearly less distant than human existence is from Divine Life. We shall therefore be best advised to start by trying to experience those facets which are nearer to human experience than the others, and only pass on to these when our *I am* has at least *begun* to be transformed into I AM, when Christ has really been born in us. In this gradual and systematic way we have a chance of developing our experience of dwelling in Him and Him in us. Rather as by taking quick glances at the sun's edge one may gradually train the eyes to endure the fullness of its light. So our belief that we are indeed dwelling in Him and being indwelt by Him ceases to be the mere acceptance of a proposition and comes to be truly experienced and felt. As our belief deepens

[1] Eph. 5. 1 R.V.
[2] John 14. 27.
[3] John 15. 11.
[4] John 15. 10.

to embrace, not only the mind and the heart, but the will, too, whereby the whole striving, active side of our personality becomes involved, so we begin to dwell in Him and He in us in the fullest sense of the word. The Incarnation, that is to say, commences in us, too. The Word begins to become flesh in us, too.

Then the servant truly begins to *follow* his Master, his Forerunner, his Saviour. Then the prospect truly opens out for the servant to be 'where I AM'.[1]

It is perhaps only then that we apprehend our fallen humanity, stripped of our illusions, and recognize our utter unworthiness of our supreme destiny. Not till then are we likely to grasp the magnitude of the adventure upon which we are setting out. It is certain that only then do we realize the splendour of our Redeemer's sacrificial Love in descending to our level in order to raise us to His supreme Glory.

[1] John 12. 24–26. My capitals to emphasize the meaning. These will henceforth always be used to emphasize the divinity of the speaker, I AM.

Chapter Three

Contemplation of Divine Peace

[1]

'ABIDE in ME, and I in you.' As the Lord's call comes to us, promising the solution of all problems and the satisfaction of all needs that are possible, or indeed conceivable, we cannot begin our attempt to respond better than by recollecting the prayer which was answered at our Baptism. (Though we may still be dimly aware of the answer.) O merciful God, grant that the old Adam in us may be so buried, that the new man may be raised up in us . . . that all carnal affections may die in us, and that all things belonging to the Spirit may live and grow in us. Nor can we better claim the fulfilment of the Divine promise to abide in us than by recollecting the Prayer of Humble Access, which is perennially answered in the Holy Communion. (Though here again we may be only dimly aware of the answer.) Grant us, gracious Lord, so to eat the flesh of thy Son Jesus Christ, and to drink his blood, that our sinful bodies may be made clean by his body, and our souls washed through his most precious blood, and that we may evermore dwell in him, and he in us.

We now face the part that *we* have to play in this communion with God. We have to believe that we *have* received what we have asked for, and which the two great Sacraments guarantee as having actually been given to us. Let us focus our attention upon the gift bestowed upon us, as sharply as possible. We have received power to bury, or destroy, our fallen human *I am* so that, seeking to dwell in Christ, and being indwelt by Him, we are reborn in the Divine I AM. We have now to *know* that power working in us. We have now to use it. We have now to experience, *feel* it destroying our old, fallen, human self and bringing about our rebirth, raising us up as the Divine I AM. Only then do we truly believe that this is coming to pass. And only then does it truly come to pass.

In the last chapter we saw how we may grow in capacity to feel ourselves dwelling in Him, and Him in us. As we saw then, the first step is to begin to try to feel ourselves in His Peace, and His Peace in us. But, as the two great prayers we are working on remind us, we have not yet given any attention to the burial or death of our human *I am*, without which even the first step cannot be taken. There can be no resurrection without the crucifixion. We have not left this out accidentally. We have done so because we have chosen the positive way of transformation. In negative ways attention is concentrated mainly upon destroying the human *I am*. This may suit Easterners, and no doubt some Westerners, too. But the average Westerner is so strongly self-assertive, so very self-conscious that his *I am* is more likely to be enhanced in that way than destroyed. We shall therefore find it safer and more effective to fix our attention steadfastly on Christ our Goal, on dwelling in I AM and being indwelt by I AM, when the destruction of our human self will proceed *indirectly*. Rather as the light drives out shadows. The strength of our *I am* will be sapped gently, as it were, without any violent defensive reaction being provoked.

We may begin this with an exercise which our *I am* is not likely to object to, and which it is even likely to find pleasing, at any rate in the early stages. We do so by recalling the Lord's invitation to seek His Rest. 'Come unto ME, all ye that labour and are heavy laden, and I will give you Rest.' We recall whatever in our life causes us most anxiety or pain, so that we may find rest or relief from these our heaviest burdens. We find that rest or relief, of course, only in the degree that we 'put on' Christ, in the words of S. Paul, in the degree that we put on the All-consciousness of I AM.

The mere recollection of our burdens in such a context may bring instant relief. Or it may not. The burdens may be of such a kind, perhaps of a painful or shameful kind, that a considerable effort will be needed to recollect them clearly. Perhaps it will help us here to recall the commoner human attempts to cope with burdens. Some of us try to suppress them. Others seek distraction from them. Others try to argue themselves into ignoring them. These and other habitual attempts to cope with burdens by avoiding them in any way, which most of us no doubt begin by making, may well prevent us from clearly recollecting them. We may therefore have to *force* ourselves to do so at first, even at the cost of pain. For in no other way can they be truly shed. 'If we say that we have no sin, we deceive ourselves, and the truth is not in us.'[1]

This recollection is necessary psychologically, not only spiritually. Why is an attempt to avoid any burden by driving it from consciousness hopeless? Very simply, because the emotional content of the burden originates from subconsciousness, and driving it out only ensures that the burden will crop up again later in another form, at perhaps a highly inconvenient moment, and possibly therefore in a more painful manner. If the burden reappears in some disguised form, and is therefore not recognized, it may well seem a new and wholly gratuitous addition to life's difficulties. And it may yield its disguise only to expert, and possibly prolonged, analysis. By which time the sufferer may have become not merely burdened but pathological.

It is therefore necessary, for all reasons, to make a real effort to bring all our burdens into the full light of consciousness, face them resolutely, and thoroughly *accept* them. 'Yes, there it is, the ineluctable fact that I dread losing my beloved, my reputation, my money in that venture. But I acknowledge and accept that dread.' It may even be necessary to grope about in the shadows of half-consciousness for any burdens that may have been poked away there in the course of trying to shed them.

But we must guard against overdoing this cathartic self-analysis. We must not allow the mind to ramble introspectively into too much detail. Or our attention may be altogether sidetracked from the next, the positive step of trying to know Divine Peace, sidetracked into an endless labyrinth of worries, anxieties, resentments and other painful emotions. We should form the habit of quickly and resolutely recollecting whatever troubles us most heavily, only pausing long enough to bring the burden out of the semi-conscious depths of the mind, and then firmly stop. Two minutes should be enough for this stage.

We then pass on to the next, the positive step in which we seek to receive Christ's Rest or Peace. That is to say, in which we begin trying to know, experience, feel ourselves dwelling in the

[1] 1 John 1. 8.

supremely restful and peaceful state which is the particular facet of the All-conscious I AM we are trying to realize at the moment. And so we begin to rest, dwell, or abide in Christ, and He in us.

As we do so, the contrast between our fallen, human, self-conscious condition and the Supreme, Divine, All-conscious state stands out in sharp relief. Our *I am*, composed of its needs, desires or aversions, strivings and pleasures or pains, stands out in sharp relief against the indestructible, immutable, impassible I AM. And then, perhaps for the first time in our life, we realize something of the immeasurable abyss between the squalor of human nature and the splendour of the Divine Nature and Life. This *experience* of the contrast is the first soft, gentle, disguised death-blow to our *I am*. For we see it, perhaps for the first time in our life, in a convincingly unfavourable light. We begin to know ourselves, however dimly, even as we are known.[1]

[2]

We now come to the actual attempt to feel ourselves in I AM's Peace, and His Peace in us. The moment we try to do this, however, we realize how completely strange even this facet of I AM, which is probably nearer to human experience than any other, is to us. What is Divine Peace like? How are we to begin trying to experience a Peace which really is Divine and not merely human peace writ large, merely the peace of this world?

It now becomes obvious that we must put off trying to feel Divine Peace until our notion, our mental picture of it is a little clearer. We must ensure, in fact, that we know at least *something* of Divine Peace with the mind before plunging into an attempt to know it with the heart. Otherwise we are in danger of self-delusion, of imagining ourselves feeling Divine Peace when we are feeling merely the peace of the world. Let us then very briefly consider a few of the salient features of that which the world calls peace, so that we may at least not call this the Peace of God.

The nineteenth century, after Waterloo, is often regarded as one of the most peaceful periods in recent history. But when the period is examined a little more closely, one finds it to consist of an almost unbroken succession of more or less bloody little wars.

[1] 1 Cor. 13. 12.

Nevertheless, these wars remained confined to various limited areas of the world, seldom lasted more than a year or two, and did not radically alter the world's social or political pattern. Hence the period is regarded as peaceful. Similarly people usually look back upon some period of life as peaceful merely because it was more or less free from major difficulties and conflicts. No wonder, then, that dictionaries define peace as a 'cessation of conflict'. That which passes for peace in the world is thus first and foremost a negative state. It is essentially an absence of conflict, trouble, suffering. Being negative, it is necessarily precarious, always liable to be shattered.

But even if by some fortuitous combination of circumstances this negation remains inviolate, it is doomed to decay. For such a negative peace is apt to breed restlessness, and itself thus brings on conflict. But even if this is somehow avoided, the negative peace sooner or later destroys itself, since it ultimately leads to mental or physical degeneration. The only really stable peace which the world can give, in fact, is the stillness of death, the peace of the graveyard.

Normal healthy people naturally therefore do their best to wring a better and more satisfying kind of peace from the world. Hence nations, groups within nations, individuals scheme and intrigue to avoid conflict between one another. They even find themselves embarking on conflict in order to preserve peace. Peace has to be shattered in order to avoid a greater shattering of peace. It is clear from even this crude outline, therefore, that true peace is in no way to be found in the world. The peace which the world can give is a caricature, a travesty of peace.

Let us now turn very briefly to consider Divine Peace. Being a facet of the Divine Nature and Life, it is ineffable and there is not much that can be said about it. Precisely because it is a facet of the Divine I AM, however, we can perfectly safely say that it cannot be negative, a mere absence of anything. For it is part of the very substance, the very stuff of Reality. Divine Peace cannot therefore be negative any more than light can be truly described as a negation of darkness. Nor can Divine Peace be in the least precarious. For there are no circumstances upon which its existence could possibly depend, or by which it could possibly be shattered. Least of all can it be liable to decay. For it is a quality, an attribute, a facet of the Divine Nature and Life, and is therefore eternal, perfect, absolute.

But however carefully we discriminate between the peace which the world can give and Divine Peace, another precaution against distorting our notion of the latter still remains to be taken. These elaborate precautions will perhaps seem slightly exaggerated. Can any serious harm, one may ask, really result from a notion of Divine Peace which is not perfectly accurate? Is not any notion of Divine Peace we start with bound to be highly imperfect?

Such doubts could only occur to those who have never experienced the immensely powerful effects of concentrating attention upon some notion in order to clarify its meaning by more deeply experiencing that meaning. Concentration cuts the notion so deeply into the mind as to cause changes, not only in the mind, but throughout the whole personality. The *feeling* enshrined in the notion involuntarily becomes absorbed into that sum total of thinking, feeling and striving which we call our self, our *I am*, and thus inevitably brings about changes in the latter's whole structure. It therefore matters profoundly that our notion of Divine Peace should be as true as we can make it at this stage. Thus it matters a great deal exactly how we *formulate* the notion. It matters exactly what words or phrases we hold in the mind with a view to experiencing their meaning more deeply. To be quite precise, in trying to know Divine Peace as deeply as we can, that is with mind and heart (as well as with will, as we shall soon see), it is extremely important to select a word or a phrase which expresses this Attribute of I AM most accurately and completely.

By far the safest course for the beginner is to concentrate upon some phrase used by the Lord Himself as recorded in the Gospels. This is far safer than using some phrase composed by oneself, which after all merely expresses our own notion, however erudite. There is no more fully expressive phrase than the one recorded in the Gospel according to S. John, in which the Lord gives His Peace to His disciples. 'Peace I leave with you, MY peace I give unto you: not as the world giveth, give I unto you.'[1] As we shall see, we may shorten or adapt the phrase to suit our particular needs later on. But not at the start, when we are trying to express the notion of Divine Peace as clearly and accurately as possible.

[1] John 14. 27.

One may remark that S. John's record of the Lord's words, written almost a lifetime after they were uttered, is not likely to be perfectly accurate. That the words we have quoted are a translation anyway. Why such insistence on accurate quotation?

The answer is that these words are the most accurate expression of Divine Peace, and its gift to mankind, that we possess. In using them we are therefore as safe as we *can* be. And that we *are* safe is proved by the experience of the countless contemplatives throughout the last nineteen hundred years who have received the peace that passes all understanding by means of these words.

[3]

We have now taken the most indispensable steps to ensure that our attempt to deepen our knowledge of Divine Peace starts from the soundest basis we can find. We have tried to ensure that our mind, through which that knowledge is channelled into our personality, is as well informed as can be expected at this stage. We now turn to the question of carrying that knowledge down into the heart. We turn to consider the actual method of feeling Divine Peace.

There is no safer nor more effective way than the one most clearly laid down by S. Paul. He tells the Colossians to 'let the word of Christ dwell in you richly in all wisdom', and the peace of God 'will rule in your hearts'.[1] He teaches the Corinthians to do the same in different words, also telling them explicitly the ultimate purpose of doing so. 'We all . . . beholding as in a glass the glory of the Lord, are changed into the same image from glory to glory.'[2] It is difficult to find a briefer yet more complete summary, both of the ultimate purpose of knowing God, or of the actual way of most deeply knowing God. The safest and most effective way of feeling Divine Peace, therefore, is to repeat the Lord's actual words over and over again, letting them dwell in us richly, concentrating upon their sense, and trying to *feel* their meaning as deeply as possible.

'Peace I leave with you, MY peace I give unto you: not as the world giveth, give I unto you.'

In this way we not only let these words dwell in us richly,

[1] Col. 3. 16. 15. [2] 2 Cor. 3. 18.

but behold, or contemplate, the facet of the Divine glory which they represent. That facet, Divine Peace, is thus imprinted upon us, and to that extent we begin to be changed into the likeness of I AM. To that extent Christ, I AM, is born in us.

Concentration is likely to be *extremely* difficult at first. Our attention will constantly wander. Hence we may have to repeat the sentence aloud at first, until the wandering, distracted mind grows still and becomes fixed upon the words. If even this fails, it may help to begin by first repeating a slight variant of the tenth verse of the 46th Psalm. 'Be still, then, and know MY peace.' As though I AM were speaking to us, stilling the chaos of our minds. 'Be still, be still, be still, and know MY peace, know that I AM Peace.' Then, as the mind gradually grows still, we should return to the original sentence, and resume the attempt to receive the Divine Peace enshrined in the words, repeating them over and over again to keep the mind from wandering to other thoughts.

We may as well face the fact that, however hard we try, our attention will constantly wander. The very meaning of the Lord's words will stimulate thoughts *about* them. These thoughts must be suppressed. For we are trying to 'put on' I AM, not exercising our own *I am's* power of thought. Our thoughts will wander even while we are actually repeating the Lord's words to ourselves. Nevertheless, something of their meaning will sink into our mind and heart even while our attention wanders. With practice this wandering is usually found to diminish, and the meaning then sinks in proportionately deeply. Some find it useful to get into the way of repeating the sentence as they breathe in, and of feeling the Divine Peace it enshrines as they breathe out.

As soon as the attention has become fixed upon the sentence, at any rate to *some* extent, it becomes profitable to shorten it. We may otherwise find ourselves concentrating upon repeating the sentence correctly rather than upon experiencing its meaning. This can be done without much risk of distortion if we remember its essence. Important as the actual words may be, they are after all only symbols of the Divine Peace which streams forth from I AM as part of His Glory which, in His Supreme Love, He eternally gives to all creation. (It is this Procession of Glory, this Divine Self-giving in Love, indeed, which creates, upholds and indraws The All.) The essence of the sentence is thus very easily discovered. '*MY* Peace I give unto *you*.' These words express the gift of Divine Peace to us as accurately as the longer sentence. 'MY Peace' cannot be confused with the peace of the world. Nor can 'MY' giving of peace be mistaken for the world's way of giving peace. Nor are we in danger of confusing His Divine Self with our own human selves, since we cannot give peace to ourselves. The shortened sentence brings out the abysmal contrast between I AM and our own *I am* as clearly as the longer one. It thus represents the essence of the latter, and can safely be used.

The question now arises, for how long should we 'behold' or contemplate Divine Peace? Everyone must decide this individually, having regard to the aim of the exercise. This is to experience Divine Peace as deeply as possible, so as to believe as deeply as possible that we have received it, and so to receive it as deeply as possible. Length of time does not, of course, necessarily yield depth of experience. Our deepest experience of Peace may, and usually does, come in a flash. It *comes* quite literally, for it is given to us. At the same time the beginner must give himself time to collect his scattered wits into the still, one-pointed beholding of Peace in which the experience is most likely to come. He must, of course, never imagine that he can *force* the experience. It is always to be clearly understood as being the gift of I AM. Concentration is easier on some days than on others, either because there happen to be fewer distractions or because one is receptive. To sum up, the beginner will usually be best advised not to contemplate longer than five minutes twice a day at first, gradually prolonging the period to ten minutes as capacity grows.

But over-long contemplation is apt to defeat its own purpose. Rather as overdoing any physical exercise defeats its own purpose. Two short periods a day, during which the effort to concentrate is faithfully maintained, are far more useful than a single long one.

Each period should always end with a few words of thanksgiving and self-oblation. 'We thank Thee, O Lord, for Thy Peace. And we offer and present unto Thee, *as far as we are able*, all that we are, all that we do, and all that we have.' Although this is given little space here, it must not be regarded as anything but essential. For without this ending to each contemplation, we are in danger of drifting into a confusion of our selves with God, of our *I am* with I AM, which is spiritual death.

[4]

We have now summarized one way of taking our knowledge of Divine Peace down into the heart. But our knowledge of this facet of I AM is still inadequately deep.

Of course it is, someone may remark; our knowledge of God will be adequately deep only when we know 'even as also we are known',[1] when the human in us has been wholly transformed into the Divine.

Very true. What is meant here is that our knowledge of Divine Peace (and to that extent of I AM) is still not as deep as it may be even at the level we are aiming to reach at the present stage. It has still not touched all the three sides of our personality. We have begun knowing Divine Peace with the mind, and begun carrying that knowledge down into the heart. But the will still remains untouched by that knowledge. And without this the whole striving, conative, active side of our personality is not *directly* touched by Divine Peace. Hence our belief in having received Peace, and our actual reception of Peace, remains correspondingly incomplete.

The whole notion of 'will knowledge' may seem strange. The need to know Peace not only with the mind but with the heart is intelligible enough. But in what normal sense can one know Peace with the will?

Let us begin by reminding ourselves of the difference between knowing Peace with the mind and knowing it with the heart. One may call the first a notion *about* Peace, and the second an experience *of* Peace. In the second case the knowledge may be said to have sunk far enough down to tinge that much more of the thinking-feeling-striving unity which we call our *I am*. One may say that a degree of Divine Peace, by taking root in our heart, has to that extent brought about our transformation. But the third great side of our personality still remains untouched thereby. The process now requires to be taken on down into the will, so that the knowledge begins to tinge, not only the feeling, but the whole

[1] 1 Cor. 13. 12.

striving side of our personality as well. It is only then that Divine Peace becomes truly *incarnate* in our personality. In the degree, of course, that this is possible at such an early stage. In the degree, to be exact, in which it has been grasped by our mind.

A psychologist might remark that it is unnecessary to concern oneself with the striving side of the personality. Let the feeling side be tinged with Peace, and the striving side will fall into line in its own proper time. For striving is essentially an effect or an expression of feeling.

True enough. But one might equally truly say that it is unnecessary to concern oneself with the feeling side, because this is itself an effect of the thinking side. (At any rate in the case in point.) Let the mind become tinged with Peace, one might say, and the heart will become tinged too in its own proper time. Yes, it will 'in its own proper time'. And this is precisely the assumption which popular Christianity is content to rest upon.

Whatever the mind feeds upon will certainly sink into the heart *in time*. But the twentieth-century mind has now grown so complex, so over-developed *in relation* to the heart and will, that the sinking-in may be so gradual and take so long that it is negligible for all practical purposes. For this reason we are concerned here with feeding the heart with Divine Peace at the same time as the mind. For the same reason it is necessary to feed the will simultaneously with the mind and the heart. In the twentieth century it is necessary to work for the transformation of all three sides of the personality *simultaneously*. Or the twentieth century *I am* will never surrender to I AM, and the new Age of Faith will delay its coming.

This may all sound quite reasonable, but if this book is as practical as it claims to be, the question originally asked still remains to be answered. In what normal sense can we know Divine Peace 'with the will'?

The answer is really quite simple, provided we draw on our every-day experience. We know Peace with the will when we cease to be content with merely knowing about it, with merely feeling it, but actually *are* Divinely Peaceful and *act* accordingly, and actually *bring* or *give* Peace to all around. A moment's reflection will reveal that knowledge in any sphere is incomplete until this stage is reached. A knowledge of love is incomplete, for instance, until we not only know about it, not only experience it, but actually *give* love to our beloved. This is the fruition, completion, culmination of knowledge in which it reproduces itself and thus truly lives. Thus truly *is*, has real being.

This stage is so obviously necessary, whatever name may be given to it, that attempts are often made to reach it at one bound. So, for instance, the merely ethical Christian strives to be and to do what he should be and do, without first having gained any real spiritual experience. He thus presents a mere façade of Christianity and is no less one-sided than the merely intellectual or the merely emotional Christian, in whom the mind and the heart respectively predominate at the expense of the other sides of the personality.

Having now made clear in what sense Divine Peace may be known with the will, we come to the most practical question of all. How do we actually come to that knowledge?

One simple way of working for this knowledge is to modify the method of contemplating Divine Peace already outlined and to extend it to practical life. We saw in the previous section that at least two periods each day should be spent in becoming still and trying to feel Divine Peace as deeply as possible. The experience gained in this way must now be harnessed to a watchword, as it were, and applied to every-day life. The watchword, which should be as short as possible, is then 'set up' at the back of the mind, ready for use whenever necessary during the day. So our watchword in this case could be 'Divine Peace', or perhaps better still, 'MY Peace'. The simplest and clearest way of describing its use is with a couple of simple examples.

The first is set in one of the many periods during the day when the consciousness is not fully occupied with any specific task. We are either merely idling in waiting for the next job to be done, or are occupied with some quite mechanical work. As often happens at such times, some anxiety or resentment suddenly floats up from the subconsciousness. We are tempted, from force of habit, to send this unwelcome ingredient of our *I am* back where it came from. But we remember that this merely ensures its reappearance at some other time, and that it can only be permanently purged or washed away by Divine Peace. We recall the watchword. 'MY Peace.' And we plunge this right into the midst of the anxious or resentful thought, as water is flung on a rag that has caught fire, allowing all our experience of Divine Peace to flood over and smother every other feeling, if possible obliterating the whole *I am*.

The second example is set in a situation in which some emotion is aroused by some external stimulus. Suppose we find ourselves offensively treated. The impulse wells up to put the aggressor in his place. But we manage to recall the watchword. 'MY Peace.' The beginner is hardly likely to feel Divine Peace in the same degree that he has known it in the stillness of contemplation. He may not succeed in feeling it at all. But if he continues using his will to keep the watchword in his mind, he is gaining a great deal. First, his normal human reaction fails to materialize, or at any rate is much weakened. Next, he is reminded of the Eternal Reality. He comes to remember ever more distinctly that I AM, the Eternal Reality, is above all, and through all, and in all, and therefore in him, too. I AM remains eternally impassible, he remembers, eternally pouring out His Peace upon all creation in boundless fullness. With this the incipient human reaction begins to die, and the vacuum begins to be filled with Divine Peace. Here the very first faltering step in the transformation of the human into the Divine actually begins. The Divine 'feeling', having taken the place of a human emotion, seeks expression in action and the contemplative, having received Peace, is able to give Peace to his aggressor. So begins the incarnation of MY Peace in the human personality, and the consequent gift of MY Peace to the world through a human *I am*.

It is hardly necessary to stress the difficulty of substituting a Divine Attribute for a human impulse in this manner. Nevertheless, there is no more direct way of working for the transformation of the human into the Divine. For what else is that transformation but the substitution of the Divine Nature and Life for human thinking, feeling and striving? All experience is there to teach, however, that the difficulty diminishes with every genuine attempt to overcome it. For it is on such occasions that the transformation most directly moves forward. It is on such occasions that I AM restores His Divine Nature, degraded through the Fall into the thinking-feeling-striving human nature, most directly. So His image, marred by the Fall, begins to be restored in us by the power of I AM, and we awaken to our true self, I AM.

[5]

The three last sections contain enough practical guidance to launch any serious beginner on his attempt to know Divine Peace with mind, heart and will. But because the art of contemplation is so foreign to the whole mental climate and over-active way of life in the mid-twentieth century, it will help him to start if the essentials of the three sections are very briefly recapitulated. He should then be in no doubt as to what has actually to be *done*. He will learn no more of the great art, let alone master it, until he begins trying to *do* what he has read about. The recapitulation, with which this chapter ends, may be skipped by anyone who finds it unnecessary. It will not be made so fully in any future chapter.

(1) We begin by recalling the tremendous fact that all the Unsearchable Riches of Christ, the very Nature and Life of I AM, are given to us in the Sacraments. The supreme Gift so far transcends our experience, however, that we fail to appreciate its meaning. We recall Christ's invitation to come unto (into) Him and receive His Rest. Here is a Divine Gift, a facet of I AM, which does possess some meaning for us, and which we certainly desire, if only implicitly. And so we prepare to believe that we have indeed received Divine Rest or Peace. We prepare, in fact, to know Divine Peace in ourselves, not only in theory (with the mind), but in experience (with the heart), and ultimately as manifestly part of ourselves (with the will).

(2) Next, we recall the exact words of the Lord's invitation. 'Come unto ME, all ye that labour and are heavy laden, and I will give you Rest.' Then follows a silence of about two minutes during which we recollect, resolutely face, and accept all that causes us to labour through existence like an overloaded ship through heavy seas. These burdens emphasize the sinful, suffering, mortal nature of our *I am*, as wounds emphasize the existence of our body.

(3) We now let the Word of Christ dwell in us, richly in all wisdom, and steadfastly 'behold' this facet of I AM. 'MY Peace I give unto you.' The quicker we can pass from our usual human, burdened state into the Divine Peace the better. For the more abruptly we plunge our human *I am* into the Divine I AM, the

more effectively we are washed, cleansed, purged. Then follows a silence of about five minutes, during which the Lord's Word is repeated slowly in order to focus attention upon the gift of His Peace enshrined in it.

(4) When the five minutes are over, we give thanks for all that we have received, and offer to I AM, as far as we are able, all that we are, all that we do, and all that we have.

(5) Lastly comes the choice of a watchword and its adoption for use whenever possible during the day, especially on awakening, on falling asleep, and on every occasion on which our natural dis-peace, disquiet, disease rises from our subconsciousness or is stimulated by some occurrence.

Chapter Four

Effects of the Contemplation of Peace

[1]

'YE SHALL know them by their fruits.'[1] Whoever has made a serious and sustained effort to believe that he has really received Divine Peace (by trying to *know* this in himself with mind, heart and will) will inevitably have met certain problems. Much as he may dislike this addition to life's complications, however, he should regard it as an important advance in the spiritual life. For the discovery of hitherto unsuspected problems marks an advance in any voyage of discovery, whether in technology, art, science, philosophy, or, pre-eminently, religion. But he may also expect all his hard work to have produced more positive results. There is nothing wrong in this. Always provided that no claim to a reward for work satisfactorily done is implied. Nor that the results are regarded as ends. For there is only one end to be worked for, and this is the death of the *I am* for the sake of Life in I AM.

We must now review some of the more important results which our attempt at contemplation should have at least *begun* to produce in us. It will be best to begin by touching on the negative results, that is, the problems. Only those likely to appear in the early stages can of course be touched on here. The innumerable multitude of others liable to crop up will have to be dealt with by personal discussion with someone experienced in the great art of contemplation.

The first problem will almost certainly be difficulty in stilling and one-pointing the mind. The beginner may well be surprised to find how great this difficulty is. Let it be clearly understood from the start that this difficulty is likely to dog the vast majority of contemplatives to the very end of their earthly existence. Even the masters of the contemplative life, at the height of their powers, speak of this difficulty. There is no doubt of course that practice improves concentration. But as we improve, so we become dis-

[1] Matt. 7. 16.

satisfied with the existing degree of concentration, and reach out further. Not to do so is really to reveal complacency, or death of aspiration. Both of these are fatal to the spiritual life, in which the *only real failure is to cease trying*.

The warning that we are likely to be dogged by this difficulty throughout our earthly existence may sound depressing. It is therefore as well to grasp its fundamental cause. This is the simple fact that the human *I am* is essentially unstable, disintegrated and, above all, transient. It is not, of course, mortal in the sense that the body is mortal. It is mortal in the sense of having to endure the pains of dying, possibly many times. Its transience is emphasized by the very fact that we are trying to shed that transience. Being transient, therefore, the *I am* is constantly moved by the thoughts, feelings and strivings involved in satisfying its needs in the course of pursuing its self-fulfilment. Its lower needs constantly clash with its higher and richer ones. Above all, its little stock of vitality, its little hold on life, after flooding to a climax, ebbs towards extinction. The difficulty of *staying* the mind upon God, of *resting* in Christ, of *abiding* in I AM is thus essentially a measure of the human *I am's* mortality, of its flux towards death. Death is really no more than the culmination of a long series of changes. No wonder, then, that concentration is difficult. For it involves nothing less than struggling out of the stream of change and decay into the changelessness of Eternal Life.

Salutary as it may be to grasp the cause of the difficulty, however, this gives us little practical help to overcome it. Indeed, we may feel caught in a vicious circle. We must concentrate in order to struggle out of transience. Yet we cannot concentrate because we are transient. Is it possible to facilitate concentration somehow, so as to *begin* to break out of the vicious circle of mortality? If so, what aids are there? In the last resort, of course, each one of us must work out his own salvation.[1] No one can do this *for* us. The beginner will nevertheless do well to heed a few suggestions for the first crucial step. These suggestions are the fruit of experience in the East as well as in the West.

[2]

The first suggestion concerns the best conditions for concen-

[1] Phil. 2. 12.

tration. The most obvious one is absence of noise, and security against interruption. The early morning is thus usually most suitable. The early morning is suitable for another reason. The mind tends to be calmer and more still immediately after waking than later in the day. On the other hand we may be sleepy. And so the best time for the morning contemplation is immediately after dressing, but before becoming involved in the practical affairs of the day. If we expect bad news, or good news, in the post, or expect the boiler to be out, or are faced with an unusually heavy day's work we are tempted to rush forth into the fray. The temptation must be resisted, and the proper period of contemplation resolutely commenced, and completed. Difficult though it may be to concentrate then, with thoughts crowding in of all that has to be done, it will be far more so later on, once we become immersed in all the detail.

The best time for the evening contemplation is just before the evening meal. The time after meals should be avoided, as concentration is then particularly difficult for physiological reasons, when digestion, rather than cerebration, has first claim on the circulating blood. In addition to recalling the watchword, we may also *try* to contemplate for a moment or two in the course of falling asleep. At this time it is best not to recall our burdens, but to concentrate at once upon the text. 'MY Peace I give unto you.' But if we are particularly tired, the watchword is as much as we can hope to hold in mind. Of course, if our burdens do enter the mind, they should not be suppressed. They should be accepted calmly, and the attention quietly transferred to Divine Peace. Concentration is unlikely to be particularly good as we fall asleep. But this is more than made up by the beneficial effect on the subconscious mind of falling asleep with the conscious mind stayed on Peace. Put simply, the feeling of Peace sinks down towards the subconscious roots of all the human, and indeed subhuman feelings which compose our *I am*, where it remains active during sleep. So the process of washing our *I am* in Divine Peace, having started as an act of will, continues involuntarily during sleep.

The next suggestion concerns the best physical position for contemplation. This is important, since the body has a part to play in the sum total of our experience. The Christian is accustomed to praying on his knees. This position very rightly and helpfully emphasizes the immeasurable gulf between the *I am* and I AM, between the minute fragment of the transient order and the Eternally Perfect One Who is above all, and through all, and in all. But the position is suitable only provided that the head can be kept in a straight line with the back, and the body relaxed and balanced. Strain and imbalance merely distract the attention from Peace to the body. In that case it is better to sit rather than kneel. The feet should both be on the ground, the knees comfortably apart, the hands resting lightly on the knees. The head and back should as far as possible be in a straight line. The body should be relaxed, but not slumped. Contrary to expectation, such a position ensures balance and relaxation. The spinal cord is as free as possible from contact with the vertebrae in which it is enclosed, and the aspiring mind, struggling to concentrate, is correspondingly free from at least some bodily distractions. At first such a position may seem rather austere, but practice will soon reveal its advantages.

The next suggestion concerns relaxation. Although the mere assumption of the proper position will be found helpful in relaxing, the beginner may be so tense as to need a conscious and deliberate effort to relax. He should take a few deep breaths, and in doing so mentally seek out every tense muscle, one by one, and deliberately relax it as far as he can. He should 'let go', and rest his full weight on his chair. As his soul is to seek rest in the Divine Ground.

[3]

Having now considered some of the best conditions for concentration, let us very briefly glance at the activity of concentration itself. Two suggestions are often found useful when trying to concentrate. The first concerns the actual one-pointing of the mind. We are normally barely conscious of breathing in and out. Let us now become as highly conscious of this as possible, and try to exclude every thought and feeling not concerned with this. We should not try to control our breathing or interfere with its natural rhythm in any way. We should simply try to know nothing but the in- and outgoing of the breath, as though observing it very closely from outside ourselves. Some may be surprised by the difficulty of this. They may also be surprised by the stilling and one-pointing effect this has on the mind after even three or four breaths. The stilled and one-pointed mind is then fixed upon the text.

The second suggestion concerns the best way of dealing with the distracting thoughts and feelings which creep into the mind during contemplation. The more seriously we try to concentrate, the more irritated we are liable to be by the constant stream of distractions wandering into the mind. And the more fatuous the distracting thoughts, the more irritating they are. Irritation, or any other emotional reaction, however, merely seems to multiply them, and is itself a distraction. We should gently put all distractions out of the mind, and just quietly go on repeating the text. Some contemplatives speak of 'looking through' or 'over' the distractions at Divine Peace, or whatever they may be contemplating. Others speak of quietly letting the distraction fall out of the mind. Others, of gently redirecting the straying attention to Peace, as one might redirect a wandering child. But these are merely individual impressions of dealing with a great difficulty which everyone has to learn to overcome in his own way.

It may be found, however, that certain distractions resist being turned out of the mind, or return as fast as they are put out. Unlike those we have just touched on, which arise from mere associational 'thinking' or from no significant cause at all, this second type of distraction does possess some significance for us. We may not at once recognize this. The distraction may merely be fraught with vague meaning and be more difficult to remove. The moment we find it necessary to *suppress* any distraction in order to get rid of it, caution becomes necessary. For the distraction is likely to spring from some more or less deep-seated emotional cause. In which case to suppress it may be the one way of not getting rid of it. Certainly not permanently. But this takes us beyond the most obvious difficulties of concentration, and needs a section to itself.

[4]

As soon as we find ourselves having to suppress any persistent distraction in order to get rid of it, we should stop doing so and examine it. What exactly does it amount to? If it remains vague and shadowy, the text may lead to its unmasking. If we are contemplating Divine Peace, for instance, the persistent distraction may be some form of dispeace such as vague resentment or anxiety. This may turn out to be the very burden we have recalled a few minutes earlier. In that case the distraction stands unmasked, and should lose its significance and cease to give trouble as such.

But it may not be so easily unmasked. In that case it must be more carefully examined. Our already recognized burden may provide a clue. Suppose this burden is anxiety about a child's health. We know this. Yet the burden remains unaccounted for. If we further examine it, we may find that it is due to the child not being a credit to us at school. Another motive is therefore at work behind the persistent distraction. In such a case the persistent distraction has been traced to some disguised form of the burden we have previously recognized.

But we may appear to have recognized and identified all our burdens, and still find the distracting anxiety unaccounted for. In that case it is likely to be buried in our subconsciousness, and the process of recalling it needs to be carried farther down below the threshold of consciousness. We may or may not be able to do this unaided. If not, we should seek advice from someone more experienced in contemplation.

Let us assume, however, that the distracting anxiety is successfully traced to its cause, and the resulting burden clearly recognized. The persistent distraction is then treated exactly like any recognized and identified burden. It is not put out of mind, that is to say, but plunged into Divine Peace. Its power to distract should gradually disappear.

All this introspection and analysis may well be unpleasant, and possibly painful. The beginner may indeed be tempted to drop contemplation altogether as having stirred up so much mud and roused so many sleeping dogs. He may even regret the passing of a spiritually myopic or irresponsible existence in which, untroubled by high aspirations, he had managed to patch up some kind of compromise with the changes and chances of this fleeting world.

In all such cases of doubt, the best way of resolving them is to take stock of the whole situation. Let the beginner remember the precariousness of even the most successful compromise with the world. At best it amounts to little more than an adroit *escape* from the worst that the world can do to him. Whereas he is struggling to *overcome* the world in the power of I AM. And he receives that power precisely in the degree that he is purged of the mud that has been stirred up, precisely in the degree that the sleeping dogs of anxiety or resentment that have been aroused are driven out of him. The mud must be stirred up in order to be cleared away. The dogs must be aroused before being driven away. The uncomfortable and perhaps painful effects of contemplation should therefore really give him joy. Even if his last state is worse than his first,[1] he should remember that this is only temporarily so. For the 'house' of his *I am* is being swept clean in order to be filled with I AM.[2] An abscess appears at its worst, at any rate to the layman, at the moment of bursting, as the poison comes away. So, too, the poisons of his anxieties and resentments, those painful features of the beginner's *I am*, appear at their worst at the moment in which they are collected together in order to be washed away. So the Lamb of God takes away the sin of the world in him. He should rejoice again, and resolutely fling open the Augean stables of his *I am* to the cleansing, purging, saving inspiration of Divine Peace, whatever the pain and the shame this may cause. He can be sure that the transformation of his *I am* into I AM has at last appreciably begun. He has at last reached the foot of his cross, upon which he must be stretched before he, too, can say 'it is finished'.[3]

[5]

The deeper search for burdens outlined in the last section should help to remove an important source of distractions. Yet these may still persist. A different kind of self-analysis may then have to be undertaken. Which brings us to the last of the conditions we can touch upon as favourable to concentration. It has been left to the last because it is the most important of all. We may call it the 'soundness of the contemplative's moral situation'. Unless this condition is present, concentration will always remain precarious. The beginner may, if he sticks to it, achieve some degree of concentration amidst noise, in the teeth of interruptions, in spite of mental or bodily strain, even in spite of all the pain the world can inflict upon him. But no amount of persistence

[1] Matt. 12. 45. [2] Matt. 12. 44. [3] John 19. 30.

or resolution will overcome distracting dispeace springing from his own shaky moral state.

The very experience of Divine Peace he has so far managed to win, indeed, will accuse him most eloquently. The very progress he has so far made will stop him from making any further progress. Which is only to say, of course, that his awakened conscience will condemn him much more severely than any other judge.

Ultimately, of course, all dispeace springs from some kind of imperfection in the human *I am*, indeed from the very fact of the *I am* being what it is.[1] All dispeace, along with all other kinds of misery, will therefore not wholly disappear until the *I am* is wholly transformed into I AM and has therefore wholly ceased to exist.

How far such a complete transformation is attainable in earthly existence is an interesting question which cannot be gone into here. The Son of man certainly declared that He had overcome the world before His crucifixion, resurrection and ascension.[2] All we are concerned with here is the beginning of our transformation.

As we persevere in contemplation we begin to overcome the grosser moral imperfections, and consequently the dispeace they cause. Other, more subtle ones then take their place. The dispeace these cause may be more subtle, too. At first perhaps these more subtle imperfections may hardly stand out as imperfections at all. They may even appear as virtues compared with the grosser ones. And so we may have to *ponder* the Ten Commandments, and more particularly their summary by the Lord, and examine ourselves very searchingly indeed before these deficiencies come to be recognized for what they really are.

One may ask why this essential condition for concentration, indeed for contemplation altogether, has been left to the last. Surely no one deliberately breaking the Divine Law is fit even to begin the contemplative life. The mere aspiration to union with God in such a situation is surely grossly irreverent, to say the least.

Very true. This is so obvious that deliberate wrongdoing is altogether outside our scope here. If the deliberate, unrepentant wrongdoer is excluded from the Holy Communion (by the

[1] John 16. 33. [2] As is so well said in the Anglican Burial Service.

Church as well as by himself), he is equally excluded from contemplation, which after all is no more than an attempt to deepen and develop the power to receive the Grace of the Sacrament. Let it therefore be said as explicitly as possible that whoever embarks on these contemplative exercises without true and earnest repentance for sins, and without being 'in love and charity with all men', let alone while deliberately breaking the Divine Law, is guilty of blasphemy, and is working out, not his salvation, but his damnation. He is heading, in other words, for the extreme of misery.

What we are concerned with here, therefore, is not deliberate wrongdoing, but wrongdoing due to being insufficiently *committed* to obeying the Divine Law. This is why this subtle obstacle to contemplation, this subtle cause of distraction, has been left to the last.

Let us begin by admitting that the whole subject is far too subtle to be dealt with here even in outline. All we can, and need, do is to glance at it with the practical object of getting rid of the most deep-seated obstacle to concentration in contemplation. We assume therefore that all of us who read this have acknowledged the Divine Law as absolutely binding.

But the question is: how much of our threefold *I am* acknowledges the Divine Law? With the mind alone? In that case the heart will remain uncommitted. It is only too possible to regard the fulfilment of the Law as *desirable*, yet not to desire this, still less to strive to fulfil it. Conflict between the mind on the one hand, and the heart and will on the other, is thus likely. The conflict may assume innumerable forms. The commonest one is obvious. We know what we ought to do, but fail to do it because we have no genuine desire to obey. The result is naturally some kind of dispeace. And the more we try to concentrate on Divine Peace in contemplation, the more this dispeace distracts us. For we are trying to experience Peace while the whole feeling (and striving) side of us is involved in dispeace.

But not many of those who seriously aspire to union with God are likely to acknowledge the Divine Law with the mind only. Their heart is usually committed as well. In which case it is usually the will alone that is in revolt. And the conflict within the *I am* occurs on a still deeper level. We know what we ought to do, and we earnestly desire to do it, yet do not seriously *strive* to obey. And so dispeace is the result, and on a deeper level than before. For that reason it is probably far more difficult to bring fully into our consciousness than in the previous case. And its distracting effects will persist correspondingly.

There is no short cut to the removal of the distractions due to conflicts of this kind. We must simply persevere in tracing each one down to its source, try to understand it as clearly as possible, and above all continue trying to know Divine Peace with mind, heart and will.

But let us assume that all three sides of ourselves have come to acknowledge the Divine Law as binding, so that we not only know what we ought to do, but truly desire to obey, and actually strive to do so. We still no doubt repeatedly break the Divine Law. But our repentance and resolve to obey is now truly sincere, that is to say, whole-hearted and whole-willed. This being so, the distractions due to the conflicts just mentioned come to an end. But this by no means ends all conflict within the *I am*, or the distractions resulting therefrom. It is only now that the *conscious I am*, with all its three sides united, may seriously begin to clash with its vast subconscious levels. It is probably only now that the transformation of the wholly subconscious levels of the *I am* into the All-consciousness of I AM appreciably begins.

We cannot, however, concern ourselves with dispeace due to conflicts on these far deeper levels. We touched on this in the previous section, when we likened such dispeace to poison being drawn up from the depth of an abscess. As an abscess is the result of conflict between some toxin and the body's protective forces, so the dispeace is the result of conflict between the mortal levels of the subconscious *I am* and its conscious levels struggling to put on immortality. Here again one can only say that most problems arising from such deep-seated conflict can only be dealt with in personal discussion with someone more experienced in contemplation.

[6]

We began by discussing distractions as the negative results of contemplation.[1] But the distractions springing from emotional

[1] See first page of the present chapter.

causes, such as those we have touched on, actually verge on being positive. For they form part of the purgation necessary for the start of the transformation of the human into the Divine. Let us end the chapter by glancing at the chief positive effects of contemplation. At the effects, that is to say, which constitute something of the transformation itself. What effects may we chiefly expect to find in ourselves after devotedly contemplating Divine Peace? After devotedly trying to believe that we *have* received Divine Peace through the Sacraments?

The answer *seems* too obvious to give. We must have received at least some measure of Divine Peace not possessed hitherto. But what does this really mean? It means that the possession of whatever degree of Peace we have received must be reflected in three ways. These correspond with the three sides of our *I am*. Perhaps the answer now seems a little less obvious. Let us briefly consider what it really means to receive Peace.

In the first place we must have received a deeper and therefore truer notion of Divine Peace. But does not the Peace of God pass all understanding? True. What has hitherto been past understanding, is now understood, while further depths are revealed as being beyond understanding. Which, in their turn, must be understood. And so on. So the *mind* begins to enter into the supreme mystery of God. Which is only to say that I AM begins to replace the mind of *I am*.

In the second place we must feel more deeply, and therefore more truly, peaceful than hitherto. We must have begun to feel, not the precarious, transient or death-like peace that may be snatched or wrung from the world, but the indestructible, inexhaustible, vital Peace that eternally streams out from I AM as light pours from the sun. This means that whatever has caused our dispeace hitherto now begins to lose its power. Either it no longer affects us as sharply and poignantly as hitherto, or there has to be more of it to produce the old effects. We are thus generally less liable to feel any kind of desire or aversion. Definite and clear-cut desires and aversions of the *I am* fade, and become vague and diffused. This indicates the beginning of the death of the *I am* and the birth of the Peace of I AM. Which is only to say that, having been born in the mind of the *I am*, I AM now enters the heart, too.

Anyone with any experience of life will be rather cautious in estimating his progress in feeling more peaceful. He will know how easy it is to deceive himself when trying to judge any subjective state. He can remove most of his doubts quite easily, however, by getting an honest opinion from those who live cheek by jowl with him. Do *they* find him more peaceful?

One may perhaps wonder here whether all this does not contradict the previous section. The contemplation of Peace was there shown to aggravate rather than dispel dispeace. The beginner was expressly prepared, indeed, for the loss of the compromise he had patched up with the world, and for the possibly very trying experience of discovering burdens which had hitherto lain apparently dormant. Yet here we are, showing him in possession of Peace as a fruit of contemplation. The contradiction is only apparent. For whatever dispeace accompanies the purging of his *I am* is only temporary. As the pain of a bursting abscess is only temporary. And as this leaves the sufferer on the road to health, so similarly each time a half-conscious or wholly subconscious burden is made fully conscious and purged away, the *I am* moves a step nearer to its death and resurrection as the Divine I AM.

We now come to the last of the three sides of the human *I am* in which the possession of Peace must be reflected before it can be regarded as complete. (Complete, of course, only in the degree that Peace was first known with the mind.) This last side is the will. For our possession of Divine Peace in any degree is not complete until we not only have a true notion of it, not only feel it, but until we actually *are* Divinely Peaceful, until we actually *manifest* Divine Peace, until we actually *give* Divine Peace to others. Until we *make* peace on earth. Until we become Peacemakers.[1]

Perhaps the most obvious feature of the true Peacemaker (who is blessed) is that he makes peace in the world by other than worldly methods. He seeks to give peace 'not as the world gives'.[2] Thus he puts little trust in conferences, politics, organizations working for peace. Though possibly obliged to organize, and perhaps even fight for peace, he knows these to be mere expedients forced on him by an imperfect world. He realizes that he (and everyone else) can truly *make* peace only in the degree that they can at all times and under all conditions *be* Divinely Peaceful.

[1] Matt. 5. 9. [2] John 14. 27.

Does this sound hopelessly unpractical? If so, let it be remembered that the world can become truly (as apart from fictitiously) peaceful only in the degree that Divine Peace, which is the only true peace, becomes incarnate in human beings. Does this seem a hopelessly slow remedy? If so, let it be remembered that the pacification of the world can take place not only mediately, but immediately. Not only through the transformation of individual *I ams*, but also through their unseen effect upon all those *I ams* who are still untransformed.

'MY Peace I give unto you.' He in whom this Word of Christ dwells richly reflects Divine Peace into the world. He truly intercedes in the Name of our Lord Jesus Christ, that is to say, in the Power of I AM. In the most literal sense, therefore, I AM gives His Peace to the world through the transformed *I am*.

The most unmistakable and positive proof of having received Divine Peace, in any degree, is that conflict correspondingly withers not only *in*, but *around* him who is Divinely Peaceful in mind, heart and will.

[7]

One last practical question remains to be dealt with here, though it is only indirectly connected with the positive effects of contemplating Peace. It will be remembered that *degrees* of Divine Peace have been mentioned. Even a beginner can surely not have hoped to possess Divine Peace in all its fullness at one stroke. The magnitude of his aspiration to dwell in Christ, so blithely voiced by the unthinking communicant, will have begun to dawn upon him. He will thus wish to know what degree of Divine Peace he may hope to receive after the contemplation of this Divine Attribute. Perhaps he will put the question in a more practical form. How long each day and how many days should he devote to the contemplation of Divine Peace?

The answer is that he should be most profoundly thankful if he succeeds in receiving *any* degree of Divine Peace he has not hitherto possessed. He must not forget his minute beginner's capacity to receive Grace. He must be supremely thankful for having received the least measure of I AM. Though I AM 'giveth not the Spirit by measure'.[1] Therefore he should not spend too

[1] John 3. 34.

long in contemplating Peace, yet long enough to give himself a chance of knowing Peace with mind, heart and will.

Such an answer may not seem very satisfactory. Let us then recall the whole principle upon which our method of contemplation rests. Our ultimate aim is to believe that we have received in the Sacrament, not only Divine Peace, but the whole Divine Nature and Life. For nothing less is meant by dwelling in I AM, and I AM in us. The contemplation of Divine Peace is thus only a very small stage in the process of developing our knowledge of I AM as *a whole*, as the Holy One. To know one facet of I AM, while remaining ignorant of all others, worse still to exaggerate one at the expense of others, is to distort the Divine Wholeness or Oneness. As soon as Divine Peace is known in *any* degree deeper than hitherto, therefore, a similar attempt to know another facet must begin. And in due course another. And so on. Until we come to some degree of knowledge of I AM as a whole, as the Holy One.

The cycle is then repeated. The knowledge of I AM thus grows slowly, but evenly. However little at a time, at least something is thus received of the supreme Fullness and ineffable Unity of I AM, the Holy One Who is above all, and through all, and in all.

But perhaps the answer we have given may still not be definite enough. A very rough and ready rule is therefore suggested. We have already seen in section 3 of the previous chapter that two or three daily periods of contemplation lasting from five to ten minutes each are quite enough for the average beginner. We can now add that he should spend about a month in contemplating Divine Peace. After that he should pass on to contemplate another of the facets of I AM suggested in later chapters. And he will be well advised to do this whether he is *explicitly* aware of having received any appreciable degree of Divine Peace or not. If he has made the slightest honest, earnest and devoted attempt to receive Grace, he cannot fail to have succeeded in some degree, even though he is not explicitly aware of this for the time being. He will return to his attempt to know Divine Peace in due course.

Chapter Five

Contemplation of Divine Joy

[1]

LET US ASSUME that the beginner has spent a month in trying to know Divine Peace with mind, heart and will, and has thus made a serious effort to *believe that he has received* Peace. Which, let us remember, is the only way in which he can receive this facet of I AM. What step should he next take? What facet of I AM should he try to know next?

Everyone is free to choose for himself. Provided he clearly grasps the principles governing sound choice. It is worth setting these out once more very briefly. They will not be mentioned again. We have seen that the self-conscious human *I am* can only hope to know the All-conscious Divine I AM in stages, facet by facet. For which reason we *began* by trying to know Divine Peace. Let us be quite clear exactly why we did so. First, because the distracted, disintegrated *I am*, seething with conflict, needs to receive at least a minimum of true Peace before it can even begin to acquire real knowledge of *any* facet of I AM. Secondly, because Peace is in most people's cases probably nearer their normal experience than any other Divine Attribute, and therefore the least difficult to know.

The next Attribute should be chosen on these principles. We have seen that suffering sooner or later drives man to seek God.[1] Yet there is no doubt that many forms of suffering also hamper him in his search. Possibly as a way of testing his earnestness. One such form of suffering is surely the bored, restless, distracted malaise which seems to be so characteristic of the normal state of self-consciousness in our age. It is the state which causes us to seek constant change and distraction, as though each minute were unendurable in its existing form.

Ultimately there is no cure for this, of course, but to destroy

[1] Page 15.

self-consciousness and to 'put on' All-consciousness. Union with the changeless Holy One alone brings abiding rest, that true Peace which cannot pall. But Divine Holiness is as yet utterly beyond the beginner's capacity to know. And therefore to believe that he has received it. And therefore to receive it. He must therefore seek to know some other facet of I AM which does not so utterly transcend his experience, and yet which calms his restless, unhappy malaise. After Peace, most beginners will therefore probably do well to start trying to know Divine Joy. As in the case of Peace, the Lord explicitly declares Joy to be one of His Attributes.[1] It is thus beyond any possible doubt that, just as I AM is eternally and perfectly peaceful, so I AM is eternally and perfectly joyful.

It should now be quite clear how successive facets of I AM are selected for contemplation, and no further explanation will be given for the choice made in future chapters. The beginner will do well to *start* by following the suggestions made there. Later on he may do better to choose further Attributes in the light of his particular needs and situation. Let us again accept the fact that each one of us has to work out his own salvation.[2] Though we should be foolish to ignore the help of those with more experience in this greatest of all arts.

[2]

We have more than once seen that our belief in having received any spiritual gift, any Divine Attribute, grows only as we come to know it with mind, heart and will. In other words, as we come to form a true conception of it, to experience it, and to manifest it in our lives. We must therefore begin, as in the case of Peace, by ensuring that our notion of Divine Joy is as true as we can make it at this stage. Otherwise here, too, we are liable to conceive Divine Joy as some large-scale version of human joy. Thus the Joy that we then try to experience, and ultimately to manifest, will be merely human.

As in the case of Peace, we shall do best to begin by taking a rapid glance at that which commonly passes for joy in the world, and contrast this with that which the Bible reveals as Divine Joy.

We saw in Chapter 1 that the satisfaction of human needs, and

[1] John 15. 11. [2] Phil. 2. 12.

the desires and strivings they give rise to, is pleasurable. Dissatisfaction is painful. It is clear from this that the *I am's* pleasures and pains, whether in their shallowest and most fleeting or in their deepest and most lasting form, all spring from its bodily and emotional structure *in interaction* with its environment. Now the body constantly changes as it passes through the great cycle of growth and decay beginning with birth and ending with death. This alone subjects the *I am* to constant alternations between pleasure and pain. The emotions *may* be more stable. But they render the *I am* far more sensitive to pain as well as to pleasure. The alternations between pleasure and pain, if slower, are thus ultimately far more intensely felt. Finally, the environment is also constantly liable to change. As each change inevitably affects either body or emotions, or both, here is another source of pleasure and pain. But whereas the bodily and emotional changes are, to some extent at least, ordered and predictable, environmental changes are hardly so at all. All this means that human joy is constantly interspersed with pain, and is really no more than an irregularly occurring series of breaks in the fabric of pain. Whatever joy man succeeds in wringing from the world is essentially conditioned, precarious and transient.

But however conditioned, precarious and transient man may recognize human joy to be, if it is all that lies within his reach, he will seek it with all the means at his disposal. Yet no intelligent human being can be satisfied with such joy indefinitely. For he will inevitably begin to detect the suffering inherent in the very uncertainty, precariousness and transience of such joy. He will begin to realize that it carries within itself the seeds of its own decay. From there it is but a step or two to the realization that human joy is itself little better than pain in disguise. The more intelligent a man is, therefore, the sooner he normally begins to seek joys that are not conditioned, that are certain and that do not fade.

Some may dismiss our whole approach to joy as cynical, at any rate as deliberately one-sided. Surely the joy of marriage, family life, friendship may last a lifetime.

True enough. But such joys are none the less essentially conditioned, precarious and transient. If only because the existence of our beloved is itself essentially conditioned, precarious and transient. It is true that some lifelong relationships may endure beyond a lifetime, in which case the joys they yield may exceed a lifetime, too. But the joys springing from such relationships are more than human, and thus not in question here.

[3]

Having now clearly recognized the essential characteristics of human joy, we may try to conceive Divine Joy with some hope of our notion not being impossibly distorted from the start. We begin by recollecting that Divine Joy is but a facet of I AM. It must therefore include Peace, as well as every other facet of I AM. We go on to recollect that I AM is the source of all that *is*. Divine Joy must therefore be absolutely unconditioned. For there is nothing upon which it could possibly depend. Nor can it be in any way precarious. For I AM is Omnipotent. Nor can it be unstable. For I AM is Changeless. Nor can it be transient. For I AM is Eternal.

We have said all this about Divine Peace, however, and a mere repetition of these superlatives will not perhaps seem very useful in enriching our notion of Divine Joy. We come to realize here, if we have not already done so, how impossible it is to describe the Divine Nature in human language. We find ourselves constantly returning to the same inadequate superlatives. Yet we have to start with some description of the Indescribable. Or our mind will remain a blank, our heart untouched, and our will unmoved. And I AM will remain an abstraction to us, and not become flesh in us. We must somehow submit ourselves to artificial respiration, as it were, so that the first Divine Breath may inspire us, when we can begin to dispense with human language.

The miserable inadequacy of human language has led many a contemplative to break out into ecstatic or poetic rhapsody. But uplifting though this may be, it does not guide *us* to the Vision which has inspired *him*. We apprehend the Vision merely at secondhand, merely vicariously. We shall therefore remain soberly and prosaically practical.

Is there nothing we can add, then, to our few rather poor adjectives in trying to form the first hazy notion of Divine Joy? Let us see what help the Scriptures will give us. The Lord, during the discourse at the Last Supper, speaks of the *fullness* of the joy His disciples are to possess. He promises them *His* Joy which will complete *their* joy.[1] Fullness is not perhaps much more than synonymous with the adjectives we have already used. Yet one can draw further meaning from the word. Fullness suggests an unvarying evenness, a maximum of completeness, a perfect integrality which is never less than absolute. The meaning becomes still further enriched when we couple Divine Joy with Peace, and call the combination Divine Serenity. The minor autocrats of the old German Empire used to be styled Serene Highnesses. They must have given their subjects a strong impression of immutable authority which nothing could shake. If we could stretch this notion of Serenity to the limit of our imagination as springing from absolute Omnipotence, we may begin to approach the truest notion of Divine Joy which is open to us at this stage.

The interconnection between all the facets of I AM is well brought out here. Divine Peace is Joy, and Joy is Peace, and both are Serenity. And all three, as every other Attribute the human mind could conceive, are but names given to the Unnamable One. Yet it is no waste of time trying to know the Unnamable One through names. For it is only as we exhaust the meaning of definitions that we come to grasp hitherto indefinable meanings. As with our understanding of the Peace that *passes* understanding, this measures our *I am's* transformation into I AM.

But even though ultimately all words expressing I AM's Attributes are misnomers, until their use has been transcended they need to be selected for contemplation with the greatest care. Because Peace is Joy, and Joy is Peace, and both are Serenity, it does not mean that we can select any sentence that takes our fancy. Therefore we should again use some actual words of the Lord in which the Bible records Him as giving His Joy to His disciples.

No words are more suited for our purpose than the ones just referred to. The Lord had just given His disciples the tremendous news that they might abide in Him, and He in them. 'These things have I spoken unto you', He then promised, 'that MY Joy might remain in you, and that your joy might be full.' It is now for us, who aspire to be disciples in our age, to attempt to know Divine Joy. And thus follow our Forerunner into the All-consciousness of I AM.

'These things have I spoken unto you, that MY Joy might

[1] John 15. 11.

remain in you, and that your joy might be full.' By using these words of the Lord we safeguard ourselves against confusing His Joy with our human joy. The more carefully and deeply we enter into the sense of the words, the safer we are against *suggesting* feelings of joy in ourselves under the impression that we are *receiving* Divine Joy. The safer we are, in fact, from the auto-suggestive nonsense of trying to give *our* joy to *ourselves*.

Auto-suggestion may be a very effective means of healing. But whatever sense it makes therapeutically, it makes none theologically and, some may add, metaphysically. For it is impossible to suggest oneself into feeling better unless The Supreme Good is an objective (and of course subjective) reality prior to the experience of it. This illustrates the fundamental difference between auto-suggestion and contemplation, however similar they may appear from outside.

[4]

We have now ensured, as far as space allows, that our mind knowledge of Divine Joy is true enough to allow us to begin trying to know it with the heart. It may be useful here to recall once more the main difficulties in the way of concentration, the main causes of distractions, and do our best to ensure that conditions for contemplation are as favourable as we can make them. It would be tedious to go into them again. If necessary, Chapter 4 should be re-read. Only one of them needs mentioning here by way of emphasis. This is the self-examination and confession for wrong done and for right undone which must precede this, as every other, attempt to realize the Divine Presence. Whoever is not prepared for constant self-comparison with the standard of Absolute Perfection and cannot face the squalor of his human nature is not fit to attempt to realize the Divine Nature in himself.

We are now ready to begin our attempt to experience Divine Joy. We start, as always, by recalling the Lord's Call. 'Come unto ME, all ye that labour and are heavy laden, and I will give you Rest.' Next, we recollect our burdens. We start as before by recollecting those which are the heaviest and most obvious. We recollect as clearly as possible our greatest anxieties, fears, resentments, hatreds, however painful or shameful they may be, if necessary making a determined effort of will to drag these skeletons from their cupboards into the full light of consciousness. There we boldly face them, examine them back and front, and accept them for what they are, burdens that cause us to labour through life like overloaded ships.

If we have devotedly tried to know Divine Peace throughout the previous month, these burdens are likely to be less oppressive than they once were. If we have faced them, got to know them thoroughly, and accepted them rather than tried to push them out of mind, they are likely to re-enter our consciousness much more obediently than formerly. Although it may not be quite obvious at the moment, these are signs that our *I am* is beginning to wilt. From which we may draw deep encouragement.

We now push the recollection of our burdens further. Let us at once face the fact that many beginners may be entirely unprepared to do so. As will be seen in a moment, this further step is far from easy because it involves a more direct attack on our *I am*. Why, then, mention it at this early stage? Because this step should *ideally* be taken here, and because it is always best to face difficulties as soon as practicable.

The more direct attack on our *I am* begins with a more careful search for burdens besides the ones already known. Most of us will have felt a vague 'heaviness' which remains behind after our obvious burdens have been identified. We now have to examine this 'heaviness' and discover its source. Our recognition of the uncertainty, precariousness and transience of human joy should help us here. If we turn as dispassionate and cold an eye as we can on these joys, we shall sooner or later begin to detect the pain that lies concealed in them. It may well be that the explanation of the 'heaviness' lies there.

At this stage of the spiritual life none of us is likely to indulge habitually in any of the crude pleasures of the senses. If some lapse does happen to have occurred, we shall have confessed this as a wrong done. Some of us are, however, quite likely to seek aesthetic or intellectual pleasures, satisfactions in work, joys in human relationships, even though our reason tells us that they are conditioned, precarious and transient. These must be examined and the pain concealed in them ruthlessly exposed. And the greater these joys, the greater will be the burdens they thus hide.

A simple example or two may help us to put a convincing finger on the hidden cause of some of our less obvious burdens. Suppose the appreciation of great painting or music is one of our greatest joys in the world, for which we gladly pay with time and money, and indeed energy. Then the fear of losing these means of our joy can never be very far from us. Or fear may be replaced by anger at any threat to them. Suppose we enjoy husband, wife, children so deeply that existence without them appears intolerable. Any threat to their well-being, let alone life, then causes us correspondingly deep fear or anger. These are the burdens we are seeking to expose. And to accept.

Anyone with any experience of life may well feel that we have grossly minimized the difficulty of such acceptance. Reason may tell us clearly enough that even these joys are 'pain-wombed'. But the moment we try to follow the mind in this and try wholeheartedly to admit that these joys are but pain in disguise, we are at once faced with the *renunciation* of these joys. And at this stage almost anything seems better than that. Unconsciously therefore we refuse to recognize the pain in these joys. And we remain blind to the nexus between the joy and the pain. So we trace the pain to almost *any* cause but the true one.

The difficulty is certainly great, and we gain nothing by minimizing it. Nor, however, by exaggerating it. The choice lies before us. And the sooner we face it, the sooner we shall make a choice that will bring us *true* joy. (And through us to those we love.) Either we cling to human joy, and hug the burden it begets. Or we renounce human joy, and shed the burden.

A struggle, and possibly a long and painful one, is likely to begin here for some of us. But because not all of us may be involved in it, it is best dealt with in a separate little section. This can be skipped by anyone who feels he does not need it. Or cannot face it.

[5]

Let us begin by grasping the essentials of the struggle. It springs, of course, from the state of our *I am*. Hitherto our *I am* is not likely to have greatly resisted the stealthy attack upon it involved in self-analysis, self-criticism and renunciation. However disinclined we may have felt to becoming fully conscious of our burdens, renunciation of these will have been ample compensation. But when the question of renouncing the *causes* of these burdens arises, our *I am* is likely to jib heavily. And where the causes are joys, our *I am* is certain to resist with all its might. For renunciation of these will threaten so much of that string of needs, desires, strivings and pleasures of which it is composed and which it values, that it will surely recognize an attack upon its very existence.

The first form which the *I am's* counter-attack is likely to take is carefully reasoned argument. It will, in fact, produce the most (apparently) excellent reasons against renouncing human joys. First of all, the pain in them will be argued away. But it is the more exalted reasons which are likely to be pressed into service with most determination. Renunciation of human joys may even be made to appear as downright wrong. To renounce innocent joys, it may be argued, can only lead to an impoverishment of human existence. To renounce joys which elevate the soul must actually lead to a degradation of human society, so that it amounts to nothing less than a sin of omission.

Some clear thinking may be necessary to overcome these arguments. For they are so much the product of the twentieth-century mental climate, the product of the *I am* in the heyday of its mass development, that they appear genuinely cogent. If they concerned human joy alone, they might not perhaps warrant very much trouble being taken over them. But they could be made with equal cogency in the face of a demand to renounce *any* human value, from the peace given by the world to the human travesty of every other Divine Attribute we shall try to know in later chapters. After all, even the travesties are not wholly valueless. Even the peace which this world *can* give is better than war. Even human joy is better than misery. We must deal with the objections our *I am* is marshalling, therefore, once and for all. (Only, of course, in the barest outline.)

We begin by repeating that human peace and joy, of course, have value. But where does this value come from? The twentieth-century humanist will probably say that they have been created by human effort. He will possibly say that the whole *I am* has evolved. We know, however, that this represents merely half the story. We realize that that which appears as evolution from below, is from above seen as a descent. Or the lesser could produce the greater.

Which is philosophically nonsense. Human evolution, in other words, is the Divine Descent. And the Divine is, of course, prior to the human. Which means that whatever relative value there is in the world has descended from the Absolute. Where else indeed could the relative have come from?

The question now arises: how does the Absolute descend into the world? By becoming incarnate in man. How else could it be? To put it in practical terms, as an *I am* surrenders to I AM, dies into I AM, so I AM becomes flesh at that point, and the Divine Descent occurs. In the degree, of course, that the transformation takes place. And this involves the surrender of human peace, joy, love, as well as every other component of the human *I am*, however estimable. If we seek the Absolute, we must be prepared to surrender the relative. For from this presence of the Divine flows all the *true* peace and joy and all the other values the world can boast. The more perfectly the Divine Attributes become incarnate, the further their reflection spreads in the world. Here is the Descending Cause of all human ascent, individual and collective.

It should now be clear why objections to the renunciation of human joy, peace or any other human values, including the most estimable *I am*, are not really valid. On the contrary, it should now be clear that whoever clings to his *I am*, thereby refuses to perform the greatest service any human being can render to mankind. Whoever clings to his *I am*, in fact, actually obstructs the highest human welfare. For he refuses to become the most direct means to this in the world.

But however cogently we demolish all objections to renunciation, we shall be foolish if we imagine all opposition to be ended thereby. Our *I am* will not cease defending its existence in deference to reason alone. We can draw enormous encouragement when we remember that it made a despairing effort to save itself even in Jesus, in the Garden of Gethsemane.[1] The cogency of renunciation will have to come home, not only to the mind, but to the heart as well, before it begins to be accepted whole-heartedly. All we can do in practice, probably, is to go on contemplating I AM as faithfully and devotedly as we can, with the ineluctable choice ever before us. Either we renounce our human joys, and ultimately our whole *I am*, and gain I AM. Or we fail to make the renuncia-

[1] Mark 14. 35.

tion, and reap the consequences in suffering. Perhaps the experience of mortals who have made the renunciation will encourage us. Let S. Paul speak for them all, as one of the very greatest of their number. 'I suffered the loss of all things, and do count them but dung, that I may gain Christ.'[1]

When all is said and done, however, the strongest inducement for us to sacrifice our *I am* will probably be, not the prospect of our own gain, not relief from our own pain, but the suffering of our fellow human beings. It is perhaps when we realize that we can only help others, through the death of our *I am* into I AM, that we shall be able to face the cross. Even here self-preservation and self-assertion will ultimately give way to self-giving. In the last resort love is strongest of all.

[6]

Let us now return to the point before the last section at which we recalled the Lord's call to come unto, or rather into, Him in order to receive His Rest.

'Come unto ME, all ye that labour and are heavy laden, and I will give you Rest.'

It will perhaps help us to make the renunciations that lie before us if we ponder the sense of the Lord's call a little more deeply. He calls us, who labour through earthly existence like overloaded ships through heavy seas, to receive His Rest. All too probably the word Rest suggests an afternoon nap, a time of relaxation, a holiday. However pleasant this may be by contrast with our normal burdened state, it is still a miserable degradation of the Rest we are called to. For this rest is Divine Rest. The sense in which a physicist might use the word, that is to say, a state of motionlessness or changelessness, is therefore far nearer the true sense in which the Lord speaks of His Rest than is our notion of a siesta. He calls us, in fact, to receive His Rest by entering into His Divine state of Eternal Changelessness. And we do so only in the degree that we deny or renounce our continually shifting, changing, transient self and put on the Eternally Changeless I AM. Fortified with this knowledge, we now resolutely attempt to recollect and renounce all our burdens and all the causes of our burdens.

[1] Phil. 3. 8 R.V.

Two minutes silence

'These things have I spoken unto you, that MY Joy might remain in you, and that your joy might be full.'

We now try to still our minds, calm the whirling thoughts induced by the innumerable needs, desires, aversions, strivings which compose our *I am*, and do our best to experience Divine Joy entering into ourselves. If we mentally repeat the words exactly as S. John records them, we are as safe as we can be against distorting their meaning, above all, against confusing our own *I am* with I AM. The Joy that we try to feel remaining in us is *His* Divine Joy. And it is this which completes *our* joy to the uttermost. The Joy we try to feel in us is thus no form of human joy. On the contrary, this is what we seek to renounce. Just as we seek to deny, surrender, crucify our entire *I am*. The Joy that we try to feel in ourselves is but another name for Divine Peace, Serenity, Rest, Changelessness. And in the degree that we succeed in feeling this Supreme Joy, so our own joy becomes full. But our joy is no longer human. It is Divine. So the transformation of our *I am* takes another step forward.

As our minds grow still, as our whirling thoughts are gently restrained and our wandering attention becomes one-pointed, we may safely shorten the sentence we are repeating. 'MY Joy . . . in you.' But only if it helps us to *feel* more clearly His Divine Joy in us. Unless this, and indeed all else, helps us to deepen our knowledge of I AM, it has no *raison d'être*.

'These things have I spoken unto you, that MY Joy might remain in you, and that your joy might be full . . . MY Joy in you . . . MY Joy in you.'

Seven minutes silence

'We thank Thee for Thy Unconditioned, Unchanging, Eternal, Perfect Joy, O Lord; and we offer unto Thee, as far as we are able, all that we are, all that we have, and all that we do.'

With the thanksgiving we descend once more into ourselves from I AM. The more vividly the memory of Divine Joy remains in us, the more easily we shall arise into I AM again. And the more effectively we shall be able to apply the experience in the hurly-burly of daily life. This is a matter for the next section.

[7]

We now come to the completing of our knowledge of Divine Joy. To the completing of our knowledge, let it be noted again, only in the degree that we reached out for when we first tried to form a true notion of Divine Joy at the beginning of this chapter. We must now try to carry our knowledge beyond our heart into our will, to the point where our experience of Divine Joy becomes manifest in our lives. For it is only then that this facet of I AM truly becomes flesh in us.

As before, the simplest way of working for this is to set up 'Divine Joy' as a watchword for daily use throughout the coming month. That is to say, we determine to recall all we know of Divine Joy as often as we can throughout the day, and above all, first thing on waking, and last thing before falling asleep, and try to realize it within ourselves as fully as possible, if only for a moment or two. So we remain overshadowed by our experience of Joy gained in our daily time of contemplation, and are in the best condition to manifest Joy whenever some difficulty plunges us into fear, anger or any other human self-conscious state. Next, we determine to seize every chance of manifesting Joy in such situations, regarding them as opportunities for such manifestation. Or, more exactly, to radiate Divine Joy into the world instead of the fear or anger or other human emotion which such situations normally evoke.

A word of warning against *misusing* the will on these occasions is in place here. We should be doing this if we *suppressed* our human emotions. Any normally civilized person exercises some degree of self-control. But this involves the use of no more than human resources. Whereas our whole aim is to cease doing this and to begin drawing upon Divine Grace. We must thus use our will, not to suppress fear or anger or whatever the emotion may be, but to fix attention upon Divine Joy so as to feel this in ourselves instead of the human impulse.

This is, of course, far more difficult than mere suppression, hard as this may be. The result is that we may misuse the will in another way. This is to *simulate* Joy. Or worse still, to foist it upon others under the impression that we are radiating Joy. In either case we continue to behave in a thoroughly human way.

To repeat for the sake of emphasis, the only safe way to use our will is to concentrate our attention upon the watchword, and try to recall the experience of Divine Joy we have gained during the daily time of contemplation. The proper way to use the will really is to *plunge* the human emotion surging up from the subconsciousness, into the cleansing calm and rest of Divine Joy. The will need do no more. The Divine Joy which pours out upon all creation as part of the eternally creating and sustaining Grace of I AM will do all that is necessary. The human will *can*, indeed, do no more. For it has coalesced with the Divine Will. No greater act of the human will is possible. As the supreme act of the *I am* is to die into I AM.

[8]

Summary of the daily exercise

(1) 'Come unto ME, all ye that labour and are heavy laden, and I will give you Rest.'

Two minutes silence

(2) 'These things have I spoken unto you, that MY Joy might remain in you, and that your joy might be full . . . MY Joy in you . . . MY Joy in you.'

Seven minutes silence

(3) 'We Thank Thee, O Lord. . . .'

(4) Recollection throughout the day of the Watchword: 'Divine Joy.'

Chapter Six

Contemplation of Divine All-Power

[1]

WE HAVE NOW spent a month in trying to know Divine Joy with mind, heart and will. Our effort to *believe* that we *have* received the Divine Nature and Life, the only way in which we *can* receive these Unsearchable Riches of Christ, has thus advanced a stage further. What Divine Attribute shall we try to know next?

As always, our choice is guided by our greatest need, yet limited by our capacity to *receive* the satisfaction of that need. But however simple the principles governing the choice may be, the beginner will do well to consult someone more experienced in their application than he is himself. He needs help to see himself as he is, stripped of self-delusion. He therefore also needs help to choose the next Divine Attribute for contemplation.

Whatever Attribute he next chooses, however, it is safe to say that sooner or later he will reach the stage where he genuinely recognizes his complete impotence. His experience and his adviser between them, in other words, will convince him that his greatest need is for Divine Power, or more properly All-Power.

One may ask if human impotence can really take so much bringing home to us. We must surely be utterly naïve not to grasp that. Almost as naïve as to attempt to live without God altogether.

The answer is that we may know our impotence with the mind but, as usual, by no means with the heart, and still less with the will. We can easily discover how deeply we know our impotence. How far, for instance, do we still try to overcome suffering with our own resources? Do we explain it away, force ourselves into indifference, galvanize ourselves into distracting activities? The extent that we do so measures our reliance upon our own power to overcome suffering.

It will perhaps be objected that suffering can well be mitigated by such means. Precisely. It can be mitigated. It can never be *overcome*. Which is proved by the fact that attempts to deal with suffering with merely human resources either leave men convinced of their impotence, or else cynical, indifferent or superficial.

Let us assume, however, that the aspirant has suffered enough to realize his impotence to overcome suffering and to be ready for an attempt to know Divine Omnipotence. His first step, as always, must be to ensure that his notion of Divine All-Power is not merely human power writ large, but is as true as it can be at this stage. Again, the simplest way of ensuring this will be to contrast that which passes for power in the world with that which the Bible reveals to be Divine All-Power.

[2]

When we consider that which is commonly regarded as power in the world, what do we find? A man is commonly regarded as powerful in the degree that he is able to induce others to conform to his will. The power of social groups, organizations, nations is usually judged by similar standards. The ways in which power is won and wielded of course vary enormously. They may range from brute force to the subtlest suggestion. Where brute force is used, the victim may give in extremely unwillingly. Where subtle suggestion is used, he may merely fail to exert his own will. But in both cases, and in the innumerable gradations between the extremes, the situation is essentially similar. An unwilling or non-willing conformity is in all cases more or less subtly or openly enforced. What passes for power in the world is thus more properly labelled *force*, and for the sake of clarity we shall call it that.

Now it is clear that force can have nothing in common with Divine All-Power. Omnipotence is not merely force writ large, but something entirely distinct. A moment's reflection on the effects produced by the use of force at once reveals this.

Whenever force is used, the same effect sooner or later inevitably appears. The victim, individual or collective, tries to assert his own will. In the case of brute force, a clash is obviously inevitable sooner or later. It is equally inevitable where the force is subtly disguised. For the will is one of the three great components of the personality and thus sooner or later seeks expression, even where it has for a time been crushed or lulled into disuse. The clash may, of course, leave the situation as it was. The victim may remain a victim. But sooner or later a change is inevitable. For no will remains constant indefinitely. The controlling will is thus sooner or later replaced by another. If only because the greater the control any will exerts, the less that will needs to be exercised, and the sooner it becomes lulled into non-use. Sooner or later the will newly in control in its turn provokes a clash. And so on. We may therefore say that force sooner or later always breeds counter-force, so that no single will ever becomes enduringly omnipotent. Therefore, force can have nothing in common with Divine Omnipotence. For the latter is not only absolute, but absolutely enduring.

Let us now try to form a notion of Divine All-Power. The importance of getting as near as we can to the truth is well brought out in the case of this particular Attribute. Otherwise, when we contemplate, we may well experience, not Divine All-Power, but brute force. Worse still, it will be brute force, not Divine All-Power, that we shall later begin to manifest. In other words, to *exert*.

When we examine the effect of Divine All-Power in the universe, leaving aside man with his free will, we seem to get little help. The complete order prevailing in the Cosmos clearly indicates an omnipotent will, but does not clearly suggest how that will is exerted. But the moment we consider how God exerts His Will upon man, in other words, brings him to conform his will to the Divine Will, we clearly recognize the essence of Divine Omnipotence. If the human will cannot be permanently *forced* into conformity, that essence is really obvious. A man can only be brought freely, genuinely and enduringly to align his will with another if he is *drawn* to do so. Only, in fact, if he freely surrenders the freedom of his will. Love has the strongest drawing power of all. And the more enduring and pure the love, the deeper and more irresistible is its power to attract. One may therefore say that the essence of Divine All-Power is Perfect Love and that it is wielded with the infinite care, humility and patience of Perfect Love.

Once we clearly recognize this fact, we can trace Divine All-Power just as clearly in the perfect order prevailing in the Cosmos.

All the cosmic movements, revolutions and processions are so devoid of violence that the unchallengeable Omnipotence directing them can most truly be described as infinitely gentle.

We may therefore sum up the essence of Divine All-Power as infinite loving kindness and gentleness. No Divine Attribute is so difficult to know as Love. Which is why we shall try to know it last. Here we shall stress the gentleness of Divine Omnipotence. We may go so far as to conceive that gentleness as perfectly loving. Let us, then, conceive Divine All-Power, not as force in any sense whatever, but as *irresistible loving gentleness*.

The combination of two such apparent opposites as gentleness and power is so unfamiliar to us, however, that we are quite liable to be blinded to the *irresistible* nature of Divine Omnipotence. The notion of gentle yet absolute power seems barely within human reach. It may therefore help us if we dwell on the omnipresence, the Infinity of Divine All-Power, for a moment or two.

When the Bible ascribes all power to God it means, as always, exactly what it says. 'There is no power but of God.'[1] We must begin by realizing therefore that there is literally no true power, no power that really *is* power, anywhere or at any time other than that emanating from I AM. 'All power is given unto ME in heaven and in earth.'[2] Divine All-Power must therefore be absolute over all that *is* or could *be*. Nothing *is*, or indeed could *be*, but for Divine All-Power. All that has being, all that lives, all that moves does so solely through Divine All-Power. Even when man appears to be and to do something utterly ungodlike, even when he crucifies God Incarnate, he does so solely through the All-Power of God.[3] Nothing more strikingly demonstrates Divine All-Power than human free will, even to err, even to sin, however abominably, however grotesquely. Whatever preposterous evil man may perpetrate, he can still never get beyond the range of Divine All-Power. Yet the ultimate proof of Divine Omnipotence must always be the *existence* of all things visible and invisible. For if God were to cease exerting His All-Power, all things visible and invisible would instantly cease to exist. Not that such cessation is conceivable, let alone possible. For God is Love no less than Almighty.

[1] Rom. 13. 1. [2] Matt. 28. 18. [3] John 19. 11.

The last point to be considered in safeguarding our notion of Divine All-Power against distortion is the text for use in contemplation. The Lord is nowhere recorded as giving His Omnipotence to His disciples in so many words. At the moment of His Ascension, however, He does so by the clearest possible implication. 'All Power is given unto ME in heaven and in earth . . . and, lo, I AM with you alway, even unto the end of the world.'[1] His presence *with* His disciples could, of course, have been no more than a figure of speech. Any spatial dimension can be no more than a figure of speech when applied to the Spirit. The Sacraments, which He Himself instituted for the very purpose, explicitly guarantee that He promised to be *in* His disciples. We are therefore perfectly safe in selecting the first part of His pronouncement for contemplation, provided we very clearly bear in mind that it is to Him, not to us, that all power in heaven and in earth is given. 'All Power is given unto ME in heaven and in earth.' Provided we very clearly bear in mind that this tremendous pronouncement is made, not by ourselves, but by I AM in us.

[3]

We are now ready for our attempt to experience Divine All-Power, thus extending our knowledge of this facet of I AM from the mind to the heart. We begin our attempt, as always, by recalling the Lord's invitation, 'Come unto ME, all ye that labour and are heavy laden, and I will give you Rest.' Our burdens clearly point to the existence of our human *I am*. Rather as pain draws attention to the existence of our body. The Lord's declaration of His Omnipotence, which we are about to hold in our minds, is an equally clear indication of the Divine I AM. The better we discriminate between that which we are and that which we hope to put on, the more likely this transformation becomes.

As always, the burdens which normally leap first into the mind are the heaviest. We examine them back and front, seeing them as clearly and explicitly as we can, however painful or shameful they may be. We next trace them to their causes as ruthlessly as we can. And we do our best to renounce, not only the burdens, but their causes. The more clearly we recognize both as features of our *I am*,

[1] Matt. 28. 18, 20.

the better. For we shall be all the nearer to the renunciation of our entire *I am*.

We now take a step further. It is similar to the one we took when preparing to contemplate Divine Joy. We then searched the semi-conscious recesses of our mind for burdens originating from the pursuit of joy in the world. And we faced the ineluctable alternatives: either we continued pursuing those joys, paid the price in burdens, and cut ourselves off from Divine Joy; or we renounced these pain-begotten and pain-bearing joys for the sake of Divine Joy. We must now search the semi-conscious recesses of our mind for burdens originating from our pursuit of power in the world.

Few of us are likely to be plagued with Napoleonic ambitions of any kind. But it will be surprising if none of us ever seeks to overcome the problems in his life with his own power, his own resources, and longs for more of that power. One may question this. Have we not just assumed that the aspirant recognizes his impotence to 'overcome the world'?[1] True, but it was also made clear how easy it is to recognize this with the mind alone. We have an opportunity here to discover how far our heart has followed our mind. *Have* we any burdens which spring from our own efforts to overcome the world? It will indeed be surprising if we have not. Though we may well have to think clearly and ruthlessly before we recognize them for what they really are.

Then we face the ineluctable alternatives once more. These burdens arise from our persistence in trying to cope with the world with our own power. They arise from our reliance upon ourselves. Or, more exactly, from the very fact of our humanity, from being self-conscious, and self-centred, an *I am*. The alternatives before us, therefore, are these. Either we go on trying to cope with the world with our own resources. Either we continue to rely upon ourselves. Either we retain our *I am*. In which case we pay the price in suffering. Or we renounce all such attempts henceforward, set out to deny ourselves, to crucify our *I am* which is the cause of all our suffering, and determine instead to seek the All-Power of I AM.

If we are able to choose the latter alternative, the oblique attack upon our *I am*, which already lost some of its disguise in

[1] See Section 1.

the previous chapter, now becomes open and frontal. Our belief in having received Christ, and therefore His presence in us, has been so faint hitherto that such an open and frontal attack upon the cause of all our suffering has been beyond us. Now we can at least attempt the attack. We must not be naïve enough to expect a quick victory, of course. The real struggle to *endure* our crucifixion begins only now. But success may no longer be hopelessly beyond the reach of our faith. We may believe in I AM deeply enough to be able to face the cost of winning I AM in His ineffable Fullness. Which is only to say that we may possess enough of Christ's All-Power to face our crucifixion.

Let us assume that we succeed in choosing this alternative, and that we are prepared to renounce all our efforts to cope with the world with our own power, our own resources. Bearing in mind the Lord's call to come unto Him and rest, therefore, we make this renunciation in each particular case. Yes, we may have to point out to ourselves, *there* is the burden. We are trying to help someone dear to us with our own resources, our own strength, our own ingenuity. And we are failing. *There* is the burden. We renounce the futile attempt to help. And immediately recall the Lord's pronouncement of His Omnipotence. 'All Power is given unto ME in heaven and in earth . . . and, lo, I AM with you alway, even unto the end of the world.' And we concentrate upon slowly repeating His words, allowing them to sink in, letting them dwell in us richly, letting them impress themselves upon us, experiencing their meaning as deeply as we can. We may be confident that through His All-Power (in as far as we manage to receive it) we shall be able to help the one dear to us.

At first we shall probably find ourselves falling into the ancient human habit of conceiving All-Power in terms of irresistible force, perhaps violence. If so, we must at once rectify the false conception, reminding ourselves of the infinite gentleness of All-Power. That it is this gentleness, indeed, which makes All-Power irresistible. We remember, too, that this infinitely gentle All-Power is also perfectly peaceful, joyful, serene. It will no doubt be very difficult at first to experience such a combination of apparent opposites. If so, it may help us if we add the words 'infinitely gentle, peaceful, joyful, serene' to the text. But the sooner the Lord's own words are allowed to dwell in us once more, the better. As soon as the mind is concentrated and one-pointed, the sentence may be shortened. 'All Power is given unto ME in heaven and in earth.' We now hear I AM speaking, but not to ourselves in particular. We try to drop out of the picture ourselves, and try to become aware only of I AM. As we succeed, our own impotent *I am* begins to be displaced by the Omnipotent Divine I AM.

'All Power is given unto ME in heaven and in earth.'

Seven minutes silence

[4]

It will perhaps have been noticed that most of the previous section, as of the sections in other chapters devoted to heart knowledge, was almost more concerned with the *approach* to experience than with the experience itself. This may have given the impression that resolute concentration upon the text, in order to rid ourselves of distractions, is all that need be done during the silence. At first this probably is all that the beginner can hope to achieve. He will find this difficult enough, as we have seen. But sooner or later, when he has achieved some degree of proficiency in concentration, he can begin to use the silence to better effect. For clarity's sake this is dealt with in a separate section. Though it concerns very much the same subject as the previous section, the contemplation of I AM's All-Power.

We saw in earlier chapters that at first one of the effects of contemplation is to stir up mud, to awaken sleeping dogs, and thus temporarily to increase, not diminish, the burdens of life. We suggested no remedy beyond resolutely continuing to contemplate. There is another remedy, however. The more practically we can describe it, the better.

Let us assume that we are contemplating Divine All-Power, and that at the same time we become increasingly aware of our own impotence. The resulting burdens flood back into our mind, distracting us from the text. It is as though our *I am* is writhing at the threat to its existence. We begin, as usual, by gently putting the distraction aside. It returns again and again. We should now stop putting the distraction aside and, interrupting our mental repetition of the text, firmly but gently examine the persistent intruder. Then we should imagine I AM speaking to our *I am*. The exact words we imagine do not very greatly matter. As we have interrupted our contemplation for the moment, these words will not be 'cut into' our mind. Yet the nearer the Bible we can keep them, the better. And if we can quote some actual saying of I AM from the Bible which fits the case, we shall do best of all. We should never forget that these words, though recorded as having been uttered at some particular time and place, are spoken to man at all times and in all places. A practical example of such a colloquy with I AM, in which the aspirant allows himself to be 'taught of God', will be more informative than much theory.[1]

Let us assume that we have achieved some degree of concentration upon the text, and that I AM's pronouncement of His Omnipotence is giving us some experience of Divine All-Power. As will become obvious in a moment, until we have achieved this it is hardly safe, or profitable, to apply the remedy we are illustrating. We assume, then, that we are aware of I AM's pronouncement at least as much as of our own *I am's* impotence. Instead of putting the distractions arising from this aside, we now let I AM deal with them.

'Yes,' we may imagine I AM saying to us, 'you do indeed labour and are heavy laden. I know that. I know what it is to be man. But be of good cheer; I have overcome the world. Come unto ME and abide in ME, then, and you shall find Rest unto your soul. For there is supreme Rest only in ME. I alone change not. All-Power is given unto ME in heaven and in earth. I AM the Beginning and the Ending . . . the Almighty.'[2]

As we listen to these words, the burden distracting us should begin to lose its significance. For we have caught a glimpse of it from the Divine point of view, if one may say this. From which it is of course unreal. I AM neither knows, nor can know, any burden whatever. For there is nothing apart from Himself, and so nothing to constitute a burden for Him. As this comes home to us increasingly clearly, so the abysmal distinction between the feeble *I am* we are seeking to get rid of, and the Almighty I AM we are seeking to put on, comes home to us equally deeply. So we learn to discriminate between the two extremes ever more

[1] John 6. 45.
[2] John 16. 33; Matt. 11. 28, 29; John 15. 4; Mal. 3. 6; Rev. 1. 8.

clearly. The ineffable splendour of I AM stands out before us ever more sharply. And so, by contrast, does the squalor of our *I am*. We realize ever more vividly how this obstructs the Glory of I AM, the Holy One in the midst of us.[1] The Holy One Whom we increasingly know, love and worship and serve. So our resolution to destroy our *I am* gains strength. Then perhaps the cross comes to call to us as to a release.

Any such imaginary colloquy must, of course, never be overdone. Or we may lapse into mere discursive meditation, and fall back from our attempt to know as we are known, back into our own miserable human knowledge. The Word of Christ ceases to dwell in us, and we are once more filled with our own human thoughts, feelings and strivings. As soon, therefore, as our *I am* has been silenced and has ceased to distract us with its burdens, we return to our text and complete the seven minutes which we have set ourselves for contemplation. We end the silence, as always, with a short thanksgiving for the Unsearchable Riches of Christ and of the offering of ourselves to Him.

[5]

Having tried to experience Divine All-Power, and so carry our knowledge down into the heart, we must now try to extend the knowledge to our will. Thus the degree of knowledge we possess at this stage is completed by becoming expressed, manifested, made flesh in us. We shall do so, as usual, by making Divine All-Power a watchword for the coming month. Let us make it, simply, 'All-Power'.

The daily contemplation of All-Power enables us to experience this facet of I AM under the easiest available conditions. By carrying the watchword about with us in the way described in previous chapters, we have the chance of expressing All-Power under *any* conditions we happen to meet in the daily hurly-burly of life. Here the depth of our *I am's* surrender to I AM is not only manifested, but tested, and given a chance to grow. As with all watchwords, we begin by determining to recall this one as often as we can during the day, and above all immediately on waking and last thing before falling asleep. Next, we determine to keep

[1] Hos. 11. 9.

the watchword on the edge of our consciousness, as it were, ready to be applied whenever an opportunity occurs.

Some of us will no doubt have found it difficult to do this, to keep the watchword on the edge of the consciousness, while attending to the normal business of the day. This is of course difficult and, like so much in the spiritual life, is a skill that is only acquired with practice. As a mother acquires the skill of concentrating on the cooking while listening for the baby's cry. As a soldier acquires the skill of studying a map while listening to instructions. So we, too, must acquire the skill of going about our daily business while listening for the Word of I AM. It should encourage us to remember that we are attacking one of the most practical, and therefore difficult, problems of the human ascent to union with God. Here is the very point of the tool we are using, our will, in working to put off the human in us and to put on the Divine.

But however hard it is to remain within range, as it were, of a watchword, it is harder still to apply it. And the present one, 'All-Power', is harder than the ones that have gone before. We must be prepared for increasing difficulties. Or our return into God would not move towards its consummation, which is the supreme difficulty of all. It will help us therefore to illustrate the use of the watchword here in rather more detail than hitherto.

Let us suppose that our work has been growing for some time, so that we have been living under increasing strain. It is essential for us to cope with our work, if only for the sake of our family's livelihood. Most of our human motives are thus in action, and our strength seems to be fully deployed. A fresh increase in our work suddenly occurs. We at once feel the impulse to make a spurt to overcome the difficulty. As we are about to react, however, as we are about to obey a habit which is not only lifelong but is inherited from our human and even sub-human ancestors, we recall the watchword 'All-Power'. This reminds us of the daily experience of resting in I AM's All-Power. This feeling conflicts with the human feeling induced by the challenging situation. Drawing on all our knowledge of God, we imagine I AM speaking to our *I am*.

'Peace, be still. . . . Be still, then, and know that I AM God. . . . You have no need to make a spurt. . . . A few more spurts, and you will be exhausted. . . . Abide in ME, and MY All-Power will solve your problem infinitely more effectively than your puny strength.'[1]

And so we give up our incipient spurt, trying instead to *feel* Divine All-Power working in us. As we succeed, we abandon, surrender our strength and our whole selves to the Almighty I AM in us.

But let us suppose that we have not been able to resist the habit, as old as creaturely life, of making the spurt. Let us further suppose that we have gone on intensifying our spurts in order to cope with the growing demands upon our strength. The day inevitably arrives when we make the one last spurt of which we are capable. We know that we are exhausted, and face the future with dread. Then the last straw descends upon our back. The slightest further effort is utterly beyond us. The prospect of failure and all its consequences bears down upon us, submerging us in despair. Now we recall the watchword. 'All-Power.' With all our determination we draw on our knowledge of I AM, and hear Him speaking.

'All-Power is given unto ME in heaven and in earth. . . . Come unto ME and I will give you Rest. . . . Abide in ME, and I in you. . . . I AM in you, I, the First and the Last, the Almighty. . . . Forget your own puny strength, which is now exhausted, and rest in MY All-Power working in you. . . . The weight that has defeated you does not exist for ME. . . . For All-Power is given unto ME in heaven and in earth. . . . There is no power that exists, or could exist, to challenge MY All-Power. . . . No effective opposition to MY All-Power is therefore possible. . . . For I uphold all things by the Word of MY Power. . . . Abide in ME.'[2]

As these tremendous facts begin to come home to us, we try to *feel* All-Power working in us. We try to feel All-Power *filling* us, so that not we, but I AM in us, is in action against the difficulties overwhelming us. Trying to forget our selves, we try only to know I AM Who is above all, and through all, and in all, exerting His infinitely gentle yet absolutely irresistible All-Power in us. And in the degree that we manage to surrender to I AM in us, despair lifts from us, and the difficulties facing us begin to dissolve

[1] Mark 4. 39; Ps. 46. 10; John 15. 4.
[2] Matt. 28. 18; 11. 28; Rev. 1. 17; Heb. 1. 3; John 15. 4.

like mist before the sun. The Sun of Righteousness has indeed arisen in us,[1] and we know with S. Paul, if only for a moment as yet, that we 'can do all things through Christ which strengtheneth' us.[2]

The situation just outlined may not seem very practical as an illustration of the daily use of the watchword. First, because such a crisis is, one hopes, not a daily occurrence. Second, because such a crisis would induce any Christian, even a nominal one without any conscious aspiration to union with God, to seek Divine help. Whereas the difficulties of daily existence are usually so small that they seem to be easily within the scope of our own resources. The temptation to cope with them with our own resources is therefore far greater than in the case of some desperate situation.

We have to admit, indeed, that to cope with the trivial difficulties of life with our own resources is far easier than to call upon Divine All-Power to do so. Certainly in the early stages of trying to live and act in I AM. This is surely one of the most important reasons why, at any rate to the religious mind, the great crises of life seem easier to meet than the daily round of 'one damn thing after another'. Even the merely human resources are stimulated by great difficulties. It therefore seems necessary to illustrate the use of the watchword in some trivial situation, in which it is usually much more difficult to recall.

Let us suppose that we are answering our daily quota of letters in our study, with a busy day ahead. The quantity, as well as quality, of the letters demands concentration. Then, just as we are immersed in trying to solve one of our correspondent's problems, the telephone rings and another problem is thrust at us. This is too much, we feel. We simply cannot cope with another problem with so much ahead of us. What is the quickest way of avoiding the difficulty? Some such reaction is probably as common as any other, and its human, as well as sub-human, ancestry is plain enough. But, just as we are about to obey the ancient habit, we succeed in recalling the watchword. 'All-Power.'

At first it may well seem quite irrelevant. Omnipotence is hardly necessary to enable us to put down the receiver with some conventional excuse. But, if we have faithfully contemplated Divine All-Power we should not have remained oblivious of its

[1] Mal. 4. 2. [2] Phil. 4. 13.

infinite gentleness, indeed of its loving kindness. It will be better here, perhaps, to spend less time in imagining I AM speaking to our *I am* than to will ourselves to become still and to experience again the infinite gentleness of Divine All-Power. The very ease with which we could get rid of the person bothering us, the very triviality of the act of replacing the receiver, should help us to appreciate All-Power all the better.

'Abide in ME, and I in you. . . . There is no need for you to use your own strength even here. . . . For All-Power is given unto ME in heaven and in earth . . . and I AM working all in all, whatever *you* may do.'[1]

And as we become still, cease to make any effort ourselves, and surrender to I AM the Almighty working in us, so our irritation, boredom, fatigue disappear. Our attention is transferred from ourselves to the caller's problem, and we begin dealing with it 'in the power of Christ'. As our *I am* fades out, and with it the emotion-distorted outlook, so I AM's passionless, changeless, eternally loving and therefore righteous, perfect 'point of view' comes to bear on the caller's problem. We are dealing with it, but not with our own resources. *We* are dealing with it 'in the Name' of Christ, with the Mind of I AM,[2] through Christ's All-Power which strengtheneth us.[3] And in the degree that we deal with the problem, not of ourselves, but in I AM, or through I AM in us, its solution is inevitably righteous, just, perfect.

[6]

These illustrations may well have made a deceptively easy impression of the use of a watchword. But only upon those who have never really tried to use one. Those who have are, if anything, more likely to lose heart in the face of the difficulties. Even those whose experience extends no further than trying to follow the suggestions of this book for a few months are unlikely to underrate the difficulties. It is therefore well worth pondering once again the enormous task the aspirant to union with God has undertaken. He will find it particularly worth while to ponder all that is involved, as far as his insight permits at this stage, in the

[1] John 15. 4; Matt. 28. 18; 1 Cor. 12. 6.
[2] 1 Cor. 2. 16.
[3] Phil. 4. 13.

transformation of his fallen, human self-conscious *I am* into the Supreme, Divine, All-conscious I AM. And whatever greater things he may see in the transformation, he will do well to remember that it includes breaking down habits which date from the Fall, and reacquiring others which go back to before the Fall.

But it is possible also to give him more practical help at this stage. We shall therefore end the chapter by underlining the point at which the difficulty of responding to the watchword is smaller than at any other. The aspirant then has a chance to form the habit of attacking the difficulty at its weakest spot. This is the moment when the impulse to react humanly (or sub-humanly) *first* makes itself felt. This is without doubt the critical moment in most temptations. The impulse must not be allowed to get a foothold in the mind. One must therefore form the habit of recalling the watchword, and exerting the will to focus attention upon it, as quickly as possible after becoming conscious of the impulse. On no account must it be left undisturbed, even for a moment. Delay enormously increases the difficulty of recalling the watchword, and still more of acting upon it. Almost inevitably the will, if it is used at all, is then used to suppress the impulse. The result may be a moral victory, but the chance of taking a step forward in our transformation has been lost.

Perhaps an example from the nursery will make the point most clearly of all. It is wiser to divert a child's attention from an undesirable object as soon as possible. Or we may have to thwart it. And so we are wiser to 'lift up our eyes unto the mountains' the very moment we find ourselves reacting humanly. Help will come to us at once.[1] So that Great Shepherd of our souls, our Lord and our own true Self, by His Word working in us, brings us forth in the paths of Righteousness.[2] So we ascend in heart and mind to 'where He liveth and reigneth, world without end'.[3]

[7]

Summary of the daily exercise

(1) 'Come unto ME, all ye that labour and are heavy laden, and I will give you Rest.'

Two minutes silence

[1] Ps. 121. 1, 2 R.V. [2] Heb. 13. 20; Ps. 23. 3. [3] Collect for Ascension Day.

Summary of the Exercise

(2) 'All Power is given unto ME in heaven and in earth.'

Seven minutes silence

(3) 'We thank Thee, O Lord. . . .'

(4) Recollection throughout the day of the Watchword: 'All-Power.'

Chapter Seven

Contemplation of Divine Wisdom

[1]

WE NOW COME to the next Divine Attribute we must try to know with mind, heart and will. This is Divine Wisdom.

It will help us if we realize from the start that this Attribute is very much more difficult to know than any of the previous ones. The progression of difficulty, in fact, here rises steeply. We must not therefore hope to know Divine Wisdom more than quite superficially for a long time to come. We shall nevertheless try to conceive it as completely as we can from the start. But we must not expect our heart and will knowledge to catch up with our mind knowledge until the next repetition of the cycle, or much later. It may take us years, indeed, to feel and act in line with our notion of Divine Wisdom. But the sooner we start trying to do so, the sooner that blessed day will come.

One may ask why we choose such a difficult Attribute so early in our course of training. We choose it because it follows the one we have just been trying to know, both logically as well as theologically. Being infinitely loving and gentle, Divine All-Power is invariably and inevitably exerted with Supreme Wisdom.

As before, we must begin by ensuring that our notion of Divine Wisdom is as true as we can make it at this stage. We must particularly ensure, and it will become obvious in a few moments why, that our notion of Divine Wisdom is not merely human wisdom writ large. The human counterpart of any of I AM's Attributes is no more than a travesty. Here it is a downright inversion. We shall again therefore take a glance at what passes for wisdom in the world, appreciate why Divine Wisdom must be wholly different, and then try to form as true a notion of the latter as we can.

A common representative dictionary defines wisdom as 'sagacity and sound judgement'. Neither sagacity nor sound judgement mean much by themselves, and so we shall have to provide them with a context. It is impossible to be sagacious and to judge soundly in a void. There must always be some situation in which one is sagacious. There must always be so many factors in that situation which need to be taken into account if one's judgement is to be sound. We may therefore slightly expand the dictionary's definition of worldly wisdom and call it 'sagacious judgement based on a knowledge of any situation'. And the more factors in that situation are known, and the better their significance is understood, the sounder the judgement and the deeper the wisdom will be.

As we are not primarily interested in human wisdom, it does not matter vitally whether this expanded definition is perfectly accurate or not. It is certainly borne out by practical experience as enshrined in a proverb. It is possible according to this, to be penny wise, but pound foolish. In other words, it is perfectly possible to be wise in a narrow sphere in which there are only a few factors to know, but foolish in a larger sphere in which there are more factors. So a man may be wise on a parish council but a fool in a cabinet. Again, a man may be a fool at the beginning of his term of office but wise at the end.

All this may perhaps seem to be labouring an obvious point. Yet its very obviousness is liable to hide its significance. This is that human wisdom mainly consists of human reactions to human situations and is, in fact, the product of *I am* and the total situation in which *I am* is embedded. The better a man grasps his total needs and purposes, as well as the totality of the situation in which he hopes to satisfy them, the sounder his judgement and the deeper his wisdom is likely to be. The deepest human wisdom must therefore essentially be the *product* of a perfect grasp of all human needs and purposes, as well as of the total situation in which they are to be satisfied. How distant such (possibly hypothetical) wisdom is from being attained in the twentieth century is beside the point. It is conceivable, at any rate, and perhaps even possible.

Now let us glance at the essence of Divine Wisdom. Our first impulse, perhaps, is to define it as perfect judgement embracing all things, past, present and future. The deepest wisdom of the world must then necessarily be penny wisdom and utter foolishness before the Unsearchable Riches of Divine Wisdom. For human wisdom, however deep, can never embrace more than all humanly *known* things of the past and the present, plus perhaps a few that may be foreseen with certainty. These things need not of course be merely visible. We are trying to see human wisdom in its deepest form. The things it can embrace may be invisible, too, and include all human experience.

We must, however, resist the impulse to conceive Divine Wisdom in some such terms. For whatever else Divine Wisdom may be, it must embrace, not only all things visible and invisible that ever have existed and do exist, but all that ever will exist, or ever *could* exist. And this is utterly beyond human capacity. When we consider this, we have to conclude that to speak of human wisdom as foolishness before Divine Wisdom is an understatement.

But even such a conception of Divine Wisdom, even one as distantly related to human wisdom as this, is incomplete. For almost inconceivably deep as such wisdom would seem to us, it still would not be Divine. It would still only be human wisdom writ large. For a conception of Divine Wisdom as embracing even all that *could* be would imply that things can exist apart from I AM. And this would imply that I AM might, so to speak, have to take account of things in forming His all-embracing judgement. Whereas I AM has *made* all things visible and invisible. Divine Wisdom must therefore be prior to all that was, is, will be, or could be. Divine Wisdom cannot therefore in any sense whatever be an effect, a result, a *product*, however complete, perfect, integral.

What, then, is Divine Wisdom? A couple of verses from the Old Testament give us as complete a definition as we could wish for. 'In Wisdom hast thou made . . . all.[1] The Lord by Wisdom hath founded the earth.'[2] Divine Wisdom is the Creative Source of all things visible and invisible. The essential difference between human wisdom and Divine Wisdom, a difference which is so great that the same word is totally inappropriate for both, is that the former is 'from below', an effect, while the latter is 'from above', the Supreme Cause.

True as this is theologically, however, such a notion is probably too unfamiliar to most of us to be of much use in starting us off on an attempt to experience Divine Wisdom. And we are trying to form the truest notion we can, not in order to work out theo-

[1] Ps. 104. 24. [2] Prov. 3. 19.

logical abstractions, but in order to experience, to feel its meaning. We must therefore find something within our experience which expresses, however crudely, at least something of the creative Wisdom 'from above'.

Most of us will have put our hand to some truly creative act, at some time or another in our lives, as the purest way of expressing ourselves. Most of us will have attempted something, not as a means to an end, as we usually do, but for its own sake as a creative act expressing ourselves. In such cases we do not merely react to some situation. We create a situation, at least in part. We may even create all of it. One concrete example of such a creative act will be worth more than much abstract discussion. Let us suppose that we feel an impulse to express ourselves by composing some verses. This intention gives birth to some idea to be set forth in the verses. This idea then leads to the creative act of composing the verses. The idea may be called the creative source of the creative act. One may call the idea the mental blue-print which guides the creation of the poem.

Here surely is an analogy from human experience which suggests, however crudely, the essence of the Divine Wisdom which is the Creative Source of all things visible and invisible. Divine Wisdom is the Supreme Idea guiding the creation of all things visible and invisible. Divine Wisdom, in fact, is I AM's Supreme Idea of which The All is the Integral Expression.

It remains for us now to choose 'the Word of Christ' for contemplation. There is no record of Jesus Christ giving His Wisdom to mankind in so many words, at any rate in words which are suitable for use at this stage. So we must search the Old Testament for the Word we need. Several texts readily suggest themselves. 'I have filled him with the Spirit of God, in Wisdom, and in Understanding, and in Knowledge.'[1] 'In the hearts of all that are wise-hearted I have put Wisdom, that they may *make* all that I have commanded.'[2] 'Counsel is mine, and sound Wisdom: I AM Understanding.'[3] But these texts are not suitable for our earliest attempts to experience Divine Wisdom. The creative, *life-giving* effect of Divine Wisdom is only implicit in them, and is thus too difficult to grasp at this stage. We shall therefore have to depart from our rule on this occasion and compose a sentence for our

[1] Exod. 31. 3. [2] Exod. 31. 6. [3] Prov. 8. 14.

purpose. We shall be able to do so quite safely now, provided we follow the Bible closely.

Part of two verses from the seventh chapter of Ecclesiastes is as relevant as any. 'Wisdom giveth life to them that have it. . . . Wisdom strengtheneth the wise.'[1] If we remember the extreme sobriety of Biblical language, we have here a very vivid expression of the life- and strength-giving effect of Divine Wisdom. A very vivid expression, in other words, of the eternally creative and re-creative activity of Divine Wisdom. But the sentence is too impersonal as it stands. It expresses a fact rather than the *outpouring* of I AM's Wisdom. We must therefore give it another form without altering its essential meaning. Let our sentence be the following: 'MY Wisdom giveth life and strength.'

[2]

Having ensured that our notion of Divine Wisdom is as true as we can make it at this stage, we must now try to take this mind knowledge down into the heart. We begin, as always, by recalling I AM's invitation. 'Come unto ME, all ye that labour and are heavy laden, and I will give you Rest.' The Call should grow ever richer in meaning for us. We have already begun to see our burdens as the very lines in which our *I am* is drawn. Do we yet hear I AM calling us to abandon self-conscious existence altogether, as the only means of finding Rest in the All-consciousness of Eternal Life in Him?

As usual, our heaviest burdens present themselves first. We trace them to the things or beings that cause them. And we renounce the burdens, doing our best to renounce also their causes. Recollecting the part our desires or aversions for these things or beings play in creating our burdens, we do our best to renounce these as well.

Now we take a step further and search the regions of semi-consciousness for any burdens which may have arisen from our lack of Divine Wisdom. Quite possibly we do not at first realize that at bottom *all* our burdens are due to this, and are merely apt to blame our lack of human wisdom. But even the greatest human wisdom is utter folly before Divine Wisdom, and not even that,

[1] Eccles. 7. 12, 19.

and is itself the cause of much of our suffering. We therefore try to renounce it as such, along with all the other causes of our suffering, and continue our search until we have found a burden which really is due to our lack, not of human wisdom, but of Divine Wisdom. This self-examination will probably teach us more about Divine Wisdom than much abstract thought. Our search may well prove vain at first. After all, two minutes is all we have for the purpose. And we must not exceed this, or we shall find ourselves sidetracked into discursive meditation, instead of preparing for experience. We may therefore have to carry the search out later at leisure. In that case we shall not be ready to face and renounce these burdens until next time we contemplate.

All this may sound perfectly reasonable, and yet have little practical meaning. What kind of burden, one may ask, is likely to arise from lack of Divine Wisdom? The answer is simple, provided we clearly appreciate the essential difference between human wisdom and Divine Wisdom, and really grasp the essence of the latter. Human wisdom is the child, while Divine Wisdom is the mother, of all things. Whenever we judge according to things *as they are*, therefore, we create burdens for ourselves.

Are we not to judge, then, according to things as they are? Are we to judge according to things as we would like them to be, or as we feel they ought to be? Would not such judgement be more fit for cloud-cuckooland than for the world? Would this not be a mere escape from reality?

Any such question of course proves that the essence of Divine Wisdom has not yet been clearly grasped. We need not disdain to answer them, however, if only because our grasp of Divine Wisdom will gain thereby.

If Divine Wisdom is the Mother of all things, the Supreme Idea guiding the creation of all things, then to judge things *as they are* must in the deepest sense mean judging 'according to the appearance', and not according to the reality. Which is precisely what the Lord repeatedly warns us against.[1] Such judgements are superficial, and their realism is human, naïve, and merely apparent. Their very humanity is their naïvete and their foolishness. They are therefore bound to land us in suffering, and to keep us immersed in suffering. For things *as they are* are effects of deeper

[1] John 7. 24; 5. 30; 8. 15, 16.

causes. Things *as they are*, in fact, are effects of Divine Wisdom. To judge according to things *as they are* is thus to judge according to effects, not causes. It is almost as though we tried to estimate the heat of a fire, say, by its smoke and not by its flame. It is as though we tried to identify a man by studying, not him, but the shadow he casts. But even the worldly-wise try to judge by essentials, not superficial externals. What they fail to grasp is that the world is itself a superficial external in relation to its Cause. It is judgement according to things *as they are*, therefore, which is in truth a departure from reality.

It should now be clear, if only in theory so far, that we inevitably put some burden on our back whenever we form *any* judgement which is based on the visible world and its values. (It is the ultimate purpose of these burdens, indeed, to teach us to *overcome* the world by the power of I AM, as well as to help others to do so.) Every time we seek joy in the world, for instance, we reap suffering. First, because we allow ourselves to be guided by effects, not causes. By shadow, not by substance. Second, because we thereby place ourselves under their domination. These shadows have become the situation in which we seek to be wise. Whereas Divine Wisdom creates all situations. For Divine Wisdom giveth life and strength to all things. There is little point in giving any further examples. Once we have grasped the essence of Divine Wisdom, if only by contrast with human wisdom, examples will occur to us inexhaustibly.

This is a hard saying, we may echo, and also feel like turning away from Christ.[1] At any rate from such close proximity with Him as contemplation imposes upon us. If Divine Wisdom lies in such detachment from the world, we may prefer to be content with human wisdom, which at any rate saves us *some* suffering. But here again the ineluctable choice forces itself upon us. Either we retain our attachment to the world, and the resulting burdens. Or we begin trying to renounce our attachment, and begin shedding our burdens.

Of course it will not be easy. If renunciation seems too hard, however, the example of the creative artist we have already drawn upon may give us courage. However little he may know about I AM, let alone *of* I AM, he regards the external world well lost for

[1] John 6. 60.

the sake of creating his own. His wisdom is human, but it is nearer than that of the worldling to the Divine Wisdom in which I AM gives being to all that is. And his reward here and now is proportionate.

[3]

As this has been a considerable digression from our immediate subject, which is the *experience* of Divine Wisdom, it will perhaps be best to return to this in a fresh section.

Let us assume, then, that we choose to continue our return into God, not finding the Lord's Call too hard a saying, and at least intend to *try* to renounce our attachment to the world. Resuming our search for the burdens arising from this attachment in its widest sense, we make an effort to renounce *all* that causes them. One by one, we review our human desires, ambitions, aspirations, as well as the things and beings around which they cluster, and renounce them. We shall probably make these renunciations reluctantly, and perhaps sadly. This need neither surprise nor discourage us. Not even if we sound insincere to ourselves. We should know enough of the process by which an idea becomes flesh to realize that here, too, time and effort are necessary. If we persevere in making our renunciations, that which reason compels our mind to accept must ultimately become accepted by our heart and finally incorporated in our will. We shall only then make our renunciations with real *determination*. We shall not find them easy even then. Our *I am* will not submit easily to the cross. But we shall at least be at grips with the crux of the problem.

Having given two minutes to this recalling and renunciation of our burdens, we then let I AM's Word dwell in us richly in all Wisdom.

'MY Wisdom giveth life and strength.'

As in the case of Divine Peace, Joy, and All-Power, we shall do well to remind ourselves here, too, that it is not we, but I AM Who is the Giver of life and strength. I AM's Wisdom, indeed, is the Source of life and strength. We, with all other things visible and invisible, are recipients. We have hitherto always explicitly kept ourselves in the picture as such. The texts we have used in contemplating Peace and Joy have themselves clearly expressed I AM's gift to *us* of these Attributes of His. Now we take a step further. We now try to drop ourselves out of the picture altogether. Instead of trying to feel ourselves *getting* Divine Wisdom, we try to feel in ourselves only the *giving*, the outpouring of Divine Wisdom. For it is this gift, this outpouring which is the essence of Divine Wisdom. In making this change, we not only aim at quite a new depth in our experience of I AM, but greatly intensify the attack on our own *I am*.

Someone may remark here that this flatly contradicts what has just been said. If we try to feel only the *giving* of life and strength, we shall surely feel ourselves, not I AM, doing this?

There is no contradiction here, however. Here is precisely the further, and very difficult, step we are trying to take. We have to learn, in fact, what it *feels like* for I AM to give life and strength. (*We* cannot give life and strength.) And to give life and strength, not only to ourselves, but to all creation. For it is only then that we experience the Wisdom which is truly Divine. And, let us remember once again, it is only then that we learn to believe that we *have* received this facet of I AM. And it is only then that we really *do* receive this.

Does anyone see a contradiction in receiving by giving? If so, this proves that he is still too conscious of himself as a recipient. No doubt this is inevitable when he first embarks upon the Way into God. Hence the earlier texts we have used have kept his self in the picture as a recipient. He must now learn to get himself out of the picture. The contradiction will then disappear, and he will discover that 'things belonging to the Spirit' are only received by giving.

But to return to our attempt to experience Divine Wisdom. Such an outpouring of life and strength is so far beyond normal human experience that even a beginning in knowing this Attribute of I AM seems impossible. Especially so when we remember that the Outpouring is to All and is the Creative Source of The All. What can the Outpouring *feel like*? Our best hope perhaps of beginning to enter into the experience is to return once more to the creative artist's example. We have already seen that the outpouring of Divine Wisdom is to be understood in something like the sense of an artist's process of creating. Let us glance in a little more detail at the way in which such a process might unfold in the case of a poet.

The poet does not look for syllogisms to lead him to the ideas he seeks to express. His ideas are not, so to speak, forced upon him by logic. What happens, surely, is that an idea surges up from the unconscious (not sub-conscious) depths of his mind, which he then tries to express in poetic form. The idea may be clear or hazy, embryonic or full-grown. But it is complete, if only potentially, as the creative *source* of his creative *act*. His idea is the very fountain of that which is to be expressed. This upsurging may be taken as analogous, on the human level, to the outpouring of Divine Wisdom. As we repeat the sentence we have composed, therefore, we must try to experience the Divine Outpouring which creates all that *is*. 'MY Wisdom giveth life and strength.' It is useless trying to describe further an indescribable experience. If the halting attempt to do so above remains without significance, all the beginner can do is to go on mentally repeating the sentence, contemplating the Outpouring it enshrines, and remain as receptive as he can to its ineffable meaning.

'MY Wisdom giveth life and strength.'

Ten minutes silence

The silence ends, as always, with thanksgiving to I AM for His Gift of Divine Wisdom, and with self-oblation. 'We thank Thee for Thy Divine Wisdom, O Lord, and we offer and present unto Thee, as far as we are able, all that we are, all that we have, and all that we do.'

[4]

Having done our best to experience Divine Wisdom, we must now try to carry our knowledge down into the will and thereby begin to manifest it in our lives. As before, we choose a watchword embodying the outpouring of Divine Wisdom. Let this be 'MY life-giving Wisdom'. We next make the usual two resolutions. One is to *keep* the watchword on the edge of our consciousness throughout the day, ready for application, and to recall it on waking and as we drop off to sleep. The other is to *use* it whenever we are tempted to act, speak, or even think in some way which is not divinely wise.

Most of us will, no doubt, hardly be able to number such occasions. It is hard enough to avoid making fools of ourselves in the light even of human wisdom. Our very humanity, the very fact of our being *homo sapiens*, will ensure us making fools of ourselves in the light of Divine Wisdom. This need not depress us, however. On the contrary, the enormous wealth of opportunities for making fools of ourselves is to be welcomed as a wealth of opportunities for growing truly Wise. But even though every single judgement of ours will at first probably be 'according to the appearance', and every act correspondingly foolish, it is none the less necessary to illustrate the use of the watchword with a few very simple examples.

Let us suppose that we hear of the loss of someone very dear to us. Our immediate natural human reaction is grief. Suppose that we then have the presence of mind to recall the watchword. We are tempted, under the impact of emotion, to brush the watchword aside. Of course, we are grieved! It would be callous not to be grieved! It might (for some) even be improper! However, we succeed in putting aside the natural impulse and the 'reasoning' it inspires, and manage to drag the watchword into the centre of our disturbed, passion-distorted consciousness. 'MY life-giving Wisdom.' If necessary, we go on repeating it until it *is* in the centre. Inevitably this, to some extent at least, recalls our experience of the life-giving Outpouring gained in the daily silences, and we try to let this swamp our grief. Or, if one prefers to put it conversely, we plunge our grief into our experience of Divine Wisdom. In the light of that experience we then imagine I AM speaking to us.

'MY Wisdom giveth life and strength. . . . You may be grieved. . . . I cannot be grieved. . . . For all things visible and invisible are from ME. . . . I AM above all, and through all, and in all. . . . I cannot therefore *lose* anything . . . the beloved you have lost is as much in ME now as when in the body or at any time. . . . MY Wisdom giveth your beloved life and strength no less now than at any other time. . . . Abide in ME, and I in you . . . and your beloved will be infinitely more present to you than is possible for either of you in the flesh.'[1]

At times it helps some people to hear Christ speak through another tradition. However alien the tradition may be, Christ shines through it unmistakably. He is the Light of the World, and there is none other.

[1] Eccles. 7. 12, 19; Eph. 4. 6; John 15. 4.

Thou grievest for those who need no grief,
The wise grieve neither for the living nor the dead.
Verily, never was I not, nor thou, nor all of these,
Nor ever shall we cease to be.[1]

And so, in the degree that our will stills our mind and heart, keeping both stayed upon Divine Wisdom, our grief begins to weaken within us. The feeling of grief begins to be replaced by the feeling of Divine Wisdom surging up and pouring forth in the life- and strength-giving stream which creates and sustains all things visible and invisible. And so, to the extent that this feeling is present in us and our experience of Divine Wisdom is thus real, our *I am* is purified, cleansed, washed in I AM's Divine Nature and Life.

Now let us consider another situation. Here not we, but some-one very dear to us, sustains the loss. In such a situation we may be emotionally less *violently* disturbed. Some of the difficulties in the way of recalling the watchword may therefore be smaller. But we may be emotionally more *widely* disturbed. That is to say, a greater range of emotions may be aroused in us. We may, for in-stance, be moved not only by sympathetic grief, but by pity, by a desire to help, perhaps even by a wish to suffer the loss vicariously for the sake of the one dear to us. We shall almost certainly wish to share the sorrow, if only out of loyalty. The difficulties in the way of recalling the watchword are therefore likely to be at least as great as before. We may even be tempted to conclude that the watchword is altogether irrelevant in such a situation, which after all is not primarily ours. Is it not nearer to Divine Wisdom to share and perhaps even bear our beloved's sorrow?

Such a temptation must be met with some ruthlessly clear thinking. It is no doubt possible to *ease* another's suffering by sympathetic sharing. But this can no more heal or *overcome* the sorrow than an aspirin can close a wound. There is only one way for human beings to overcome suffering. That is by getting rid of their *I am* and putting on I AM Who alone has overcome the world. We can no more *really* help them by pitying them than we can help ourselves in a similar situation by self-pity. And this is particularly so if they know nothing of the mysteries we are dis-

[1] Krishna's words.

cussing. Or, if they do, are too shaken by grief to act on their knowledge.

Firmly putting away our pity, therefore, we determine to put our generous impulse to help to better use, and resolutely recall the watchword. Next we do our best to recall our experience of life- and strength-giving Divine Wisdom. Then we plunge all the complex emotions surrounding our grief-stricken beloved into the Divine Outpouring. If necessary, we may imaginatively hear I AM speaking to us again. For the situation we are in is precisely the same here as in the previous illustration. Our object is, as always, to cease feeling humanly and to begin feeling divinely. First for our own sakes. Or we lack real power to help. Then for the sake of our beloved. For it is only to the extent that the transformation takes place in us that we receive power to help, not only ourselves, but others. 'For without ME ye can do nothing.'[1] Then, when some measure of Divine Wisdom is present in us, we may specifically remember our beloved, with every hope of being able to give real help. For it will be, not our pity, not even our wish to bear another's sorrow, but Divine Wisdom that will give the help, together with life and strength, and all the other Unsearchable Riches of Christ.

It will be best to end our illustration of the use of the watchword with an example of quite another kind. Let us suppose that some admired friend of ours suddenly proves to be quite unworthy. We are deeply shocked. Not only by the offence. But also by the fact that *our* friend is the offender. And possibly most of all because our knowledge of character has proved so very poor. The whole situation, all the details of our friend's unworthy behaviour, thoroughly repels us.

Let us suppose, however, that we manage to recall the watchword. For a beginner this would be a considerable feat. The watchword reminds us that repulsion has no place in Divine Wisdom. We remember that we are judging according to the appearance, according to effects. Not only is our view of the situation thus utterly superficial. But, worse still, our judgement is the product of the repellent situation spread out before us, with the result that we are under its influence. Whereas Divine Wisdom is in no sense a product, but is the Creative Source of all things. Instead of

[1] John 15. 5.

being under the influence of anything, I AM is the Supreme Cause of all things. And, the Cause being perfect, all things must *in their essence* be perfect, too. We then try to know our fallen friend in his *essential* perfection.

Nothing could be more difficult. (Except to love him in his repellent state; but that is a subject for the next chapter.) It may therefore help us to see him from I AM's point of view, with the Wisdom from above, if we glance at the process by which he must ultimately achieve his perfection. As all mankind ultimately must. His fall inevitably brings him the appropriate suffering. It has already begun to do so. He may refuse to learn from this for a time. But sooner or later he will be driven to learn the Way into God. For there is no other way out of suffering. And so his suffering purifies him. If not in earthly existence, then in some subsequent one. And we try to know our friend, our fallen friend, in his purified and perfected state. We try to know him as I AM knows him, us, and all creation.

We cannot realize too clearly that we succeed in this only in the degree that our repulsion is washed in Divine Wisdom. In the degree that we feel Divine Wisdom instead of repulsion, precisely in the same degree are we able to know our fallen friend in his essential perfection. For his essential perfection is nothing but the product of the same life- and strength-giving Wisdom that we are trying to know in ourselves. And know, let it be remembered, not only with our mind, but with our heart, and with our will.

We are the first to benefit by this knowledge. Who would not prefer to be filled with Wisdom rather than with repulsion? Our fallen friend is the next to receive help. For in the degree that, by Divine Wisdom in us, we know him in his essential perfection, he awakens to this too. So, instead of mentally leaving him embedded in his fallen state, we are able to help him creatively.

[5]

The Anglo-Saxon ordinarily is among the practical Christians. If he concerns himself with his own personal salvation, he usually inclines to see this largely as the fruit of good works. In spite of all that the New Testament says to the contrary. It has been remarked that Pelagianism has always been endemic in English

Christianity. Perhaps this is the inevitable result of the strong streak of self-assertiveness and self-reliance in the Anglo-Saxon. Doubts may therefore have lurked in some of us, even up to this stage, that our contemplative exercises may be 'self-centred'. Although our constantly repeated aim is to get rid of the self, we may by some strange process of reasoning have suspected that we are doing this for our own benefit. Do we not put ourselves first, both in the contemplative silences, and in the use of watchwords?

If any such doubts have lingered, they should finally have been dispelled in the last two illustrations of the use of the watchword. It must surely be clear beyond any possible doubt that we receive help for ourselves both *by* helping another and *in order* to help him. Only one such 'third party' was mentioned in each illustration. The help that other human beings also receive whenever we seek help for ourselves is past calculation. Whenever we explicitly 'remember before God' all our fellow-human beings, use our human mind to recall all our fellow-human beings before I AM in us, the help we render is world-wide. For the majority of them know nothing of the only way of overcoming the world and its pain. And whatever the minority may know of this in theory, it is certain that very few know how to apply the theory in the mid-twentieth century. Or if they do, may well lack the resolution to face the cross. In the degree that we receive the Unsearchable Riches of Christ, in the same degree are we capable of mediating them to all other human beings who are as yet without power to receive them themselves.

[6]

Summary of the daily exercise

(1) 'Come unto ME, all ye that labour and are heavy laden, and I will give you Rest.'

Two minutes silence

(2) 'MY wisdom giveth life and strength.'

Ten minutes silence

(3) 'We thank Thee, O Lord. . . .'

(4) Recollection throughout the day of the watchword: 'MY life-giving Wisdom.'

Chapter Eight

Contemplation of Divine Love

[1]

We now come to the last of the Divine Attributes which the scope of this book allows us to deal with. This is Divine Love. As we have seen more than once, no other Attribute is further removed from normal human experience. It is, in fact, hardly correct to speak of Divine Love as an Attribute at all. For God is Love.[1] Divine Love is more properly, therefore, seen as the very essence of God. We may perhaps call it the perfection of God in its dynamic form.

One may ask, here again, why so difficult a subject for contemplation is put before beginners. The answer is much the same as before. It is worth repeating none the less. Even though the system of training outlined here is intended for beginners, it is also designed to carry them much farther by constantly bringing them back to the contemplation of the same few fundamental Attributes, the same few fundamental facets of I AM. One reason for regarding Divine Love as fundamental has just been suggested. We now add that, as Divine Wisdom follows logically and theologically on Divine All-Power, so Divine Love similarly follows on Divine Wisdom. If Divine All-Power is invariably exerted with supreme Wisdom, then Divine Wisdom is invariably supremely loving.

Our first task, as always, is to ensure that our notion of Divine Love is as true as we can make it at this stage. As before, the simplest way of doing so is to glance first at human love, at what passes for love among human beings, realize clearly why Divine Love must be essentially different, and then try to conceive the latter.

When we consider the innumerable forms that love takes among human beings, we have to conclude that no two forms can be

[1] 1 John 4. 8.

exactly alike. For love is that through which an individual finally expresses himself and fulfils himself at whatever high-water mark of development he has reached. And this will naturally and necessarily vary. So at one end of the scale we find self-giving on the level of body. We see here a person fulfilling himself merely as a conscious physical organism. At the other end of the scale we find self-giving on the level of psyche. We see here a person fulfilling himself as that immensely complex string of thoughts, feelings and strivings which composes the self-conscious *I am*. The love at one end of the scale will therefore be 'fleshly', and at the other 'intellectual'.

Whether such extremes are ever found in practice is beside the point here. They are mentioned merely to delimit one aspect of human nature, a subject, let it be remembered, which is second in profundity only to that of the Divine Nature. The great mass of mankind is certainly to be found in every stage of development between these two (possibly hypothetical) extremes, so that the love of each individual is a unique mixture of fleshliness and intellect. The primitive, merely conscious, man's love will no doubt appear carnal bestiality to his self-conscious brother. While the latter probably strikes the former as an overweening, emasculated highbrow who, when he does respond to his flesh, is all too prone to overwork it to extremes.

But even though no two kinds of self-giving among human beings are exactly alike, we find that all share one essential characteristic. All forms of human love depend upon some object for their activity. All are essentially responses to some object that attracts them. Desire, in its comprehensive sense of positive appetency, is thus an integral part of all human self-giving. When a man says 'I love', he means that he desires the one who attracts him. When a mother gives up all for her child, which may be an ugly duckling to everyone else, and all the more attractive to her for that reason, it only means that she desires its good. When a thinker says he will die in order to impart his ideas for mankind's benefit, it means that the good of mankind attracts him more than his own existence.

All this may sound like a depreciation of human love. And when that love is genuinely self-sacrificing, the depreciation may seem not only cynical but actually erroneous. Has not the Lord Himself declared that no man has greater love than to lay down his life for his friends?[1]

No depreciation is intended. All we are trying to do is to see as clearly as possible the essence of human love. And this is, quite undeniably, that if there is no beloved there is no self-giving, no love. It is so logically as well as psychologically. Where there is no beloved, there can logically be no lover. Where the beloved ceases to attract, there can psychologically be no lover. Where there is no friend, there can be no laying down of life for his sake. Let us be perfectly clear on this point, failure to appreciate which merely clouds the whole subject with sentimentality. And what is worse, we shall never grasp the essential distinction between human love and Divine Love, and therefore never form a true notion of the latter.

Now let us turn to Divine Love. If the essence of human love is desire, response to an object's attraction, what is the essence of Divine Love? It will help us to begin to grasp that essence if we remember the fundamental distinction between human wisdom and Divine Wisdom. As we saw in the previous chapter, the first is an effect, while the second is causal. The distinction between human love and Divine Love must be similar. Let us turn to the Bible for clear light on the subject. S. John, whose knowledge of this must have rivalled that of S. Paul and overshadowed that of almost any other human being, gives us a key to the answer we seek. 'Herein is love,' he writes, meaning real, true, in short, Divine Love, 'not that we loved God, but that he loved us.'[2]

These words first of all clearly confirm what we already infer, that is that human love is essentially distinct from Divine Love. The latter is unlikely, therefore, to be tinctured with desire, unlikely to be response to some attractive object. What is there in existence, indeed, that could possibly *attract* God? One might reply that, being made good, creation must in some sense be attractive. This *might* apply to the Cosmos, but hardly to man who has fallen from the original state of goodness in which he was created. Man, steeped in all the squalor of his fallen humanity, is frequently repellent even to man himself, at any rate in his most lucid moments.

This reason may sound slightly flippant, however, and so we

[1] John 15. 13. [2] 1 John 4. 10.

turn to a more solid one. It is implicit in the distinction between human wisdom and Divine Wisdom. S. John helps us again explicitly. 'We love Him', he writes, 'because *He first loved us*.'[1] This tells us that Divine Love cannot be desire for objects, response to the attraction of objects, not only because none seems worthy of attracting God, but simply because God loved before any object whatever existed at all. And, of course, it must be so. God is the Supreme Cause of The All. God also is Love. He must therefore have loved before the beginning of all things, and will continue to love after their ending. His Love must indeed be the very origin of that creativity which has called The All forth out of nothing. His Loving must be the very essence, the very spearhead of His Creating.[2]

Now if God's Love has created The All, it must also uphold The All. Or The All would not continue to exist. And not only does Divine Love uphold The All, but as we shall see in a moment, it redeems whatever portion of The All has fallen from its pristine goodness. And, finally, as we shall see, it is Divine Love that draws all things back to God, gathering them together again in One.[3] What else but Divine Love could accomplish all this, which is no less creative than the original making of all things visible and invisible?

It should now be clear why the distinction between human love and wisdom on the one hand, and Divine Love and Wisdom on the other, is similar. Where the human is an effect, the Divine is supremely causal. But Divine Wisdom is not synonymous with Divine Love. This was made clear earlier in the chapter. Both form part of Divine Creativity, but play different parts therein. We need not go into this more fully now. We shall do so more appropriately in the next chapter.

[2]

All that has been said on the subject of Divine Love is no doubt theologically sound. Our purpose here, however, is to form the truest notion we can of Divine Love, not for its own sake alone, but also in order to provide a springboard for experience. What can Divine Love be like as an experience? If, being the opposite pole of human love, Divine Love is utterly devoid of all desire,

[1] 1 John 4. 19. (My italics.) [2] John 17. 24. [3] John 12. 32; 11. 52; Eph. 1. 10.

what is its 'feeling content'? What does it 'feel like' to love Divinely? To love irrespective of the attraction or repulsion of an object? To love, indeed, without an object at all?

Again S. John points us to the answer, quoting the Lord. 'God so loved the world, that He gave His only begotten Son . . . that the world through Him might be saved.'[1] The Son is, of course, God Himself in His objective, manifested, expressed aspect: the Word of God. We may therefore slightly paraphrase S. John and say that God so loved the world that He gave Himself for its salvation. We need not go fully into the meaning of the salvation of the world. Let us here simply regard salvation as the greatest possible good of the world. God, having brought The All into being through His Self-giving, also gave Himself for the salvation of that part of His Creation which needed saving. Having given the greatest possible benefit of perfect existence to The All, He restored this good to that part of The All which had fallen from it. The 'feeling content' of Divine Love may therefore be defined as self-sacrifice, self-spending, self-giving, or better still as sacrificial self-giving for the greatest possible good of the beloved, without condition, reserve or limit.

S. Paul's ode to Love may help some of us to clothe this very bare definition with more meaning.[2] But most of us will probably find the Passion, culminating in the Crucifixion, the most detailed, accurate, and above all practical, illustration of Divine Self-giving in Love. We shall find it most rewarding of all, therefore, simply to 'survey the wondrous Cross'. There we see an act of self-sacrifice for the greatest possible good of mankind. There we see Divine Love which, having created all things including man, redeems man from his fall. No other motive whatever enters into the sacrificial act. There is no demand for reciprocity. No conditions, reservations or limits are imposed. The Sacrifice is made unasked for, unaccepted and unvalued. It is made because it 'must' be made. God is Love, and 'cannot' but make the Sacrifice. For His Self-sacrifice, His Self-spending, His Self-giving is nothing but His Self-expression, the dynamic aspect of His Eternal Perfection as the Source and Goal of The All.

As a flash of lightning is a momentary exemplar of the most brilliant earthly light, so the Cross revealed at a certain point in

[1] John 3. 16, 17. [2] 1 Cor. 13.

time and space the actual *way* in which God makes, upholds, redeems and gathers together again in One all things visible and invisible. As a flash of lightning is a momentary exemplar of blinding light, so the Cross is a symbol of the humanly incomprehensible Eternal Procession and Return of Divine Love through which The All is eternally projected and gathered together again in One. The Cross reveals the method which God uses in bringing about the Beginning and the Ending of all things visible and invisible. 'I AM Alpha and Omega, the Beginning and the Ending . . . the Almighty.'[1]

As the sacrificial quality of Divine Love begins to come home to us, we may well begin finding excuses for avoiding any experience of such a kind. Can a man really break out of his human limitations to such an extent? Is unconditional self-giving really possible in the world? Is it even right? Do we not pervert our fellow-human beings, for instance, by unconditionally giving in to them? Does not justice, and indeed the whole Divine Cause in the world, suffer thereby?

We must remember, however, that God sacrifices, spends, gives Himself for no purpose but to confer the *supreme benefit* upon man. When man abuses the Gift, he does not benefit. And so it is then that Divine Love confronts him as Wrath. The resulting suffering is the very means by which Divine Love purges man and fits him to partake of Divine Holiness.[2] This is the supreme benefit.

Do we hear the word 'wrath' with relief? Are we justified, then, in displaying wrath on occasions?

The answer is that we are justified in displaying wrath only in the degree that we are able to display Divine Love. As we are able to bear the Cross, in other words, so we become fit to manifest Divine Wrath. How else could it be? Do we not put on *any* facet of I AM only in so far as we get rid of our own *I am*?

But when all is said and done, and much more can be said and done, the Lord has left no one who aspires to be His disciple in doubt on the matter. 'This is MY commandment, that ye love one another, as I have loved you.'[3] Whoever aspires to follow Jesus Christ into God must learn to love as He loves. He may no longer be content to love his neighbour *as himself*. He must learn to love as I AM loves. It is inconceivable that God should mock man by

[1] Rev. 1. 8. [2] Heb. 12. 10. [3] John 15. 12.

calling upon him to do what is impossible. Or what is in any way wrong.

The Cross, then, is the simplest yet most complete summary of our notion of Divine Love. So it is that a well-known traditional way of contemplating Divine Love is to contemplate the actual Crucifix, literally to 'survey the wondrous Cross'. Very roughly speaking, one begins by trying to imagine the Lord's bodily and mental suffering on the Cross, and goes on to try and share these oneself. One tries to imagine oneself upon the Cross.

We shall not follow this method, however. It is not strictly Biblical, and is thus open to danger. Following S. Paul we aspire to know Christ, not after the flesh, but after the Spirit.[1] How else can we put on Jesus Christ Who is the same yesterday, today and forever?[2] We aspire to a knowledge of Divine Love which reaches beyond symbols to the reality.

To contemplate the symbol, however, is not merely second-best. It might actually hinder us from knowing the Reality of Divine Love. The symbol is charged with such enormous emotional significance that we might easily sentimentalize Divine Love. We might, for instance, be so impressed by the sacrifice for *our* sakes as to make no effort to sacrifice ourselves for the sake of *others*. Or we might exalt its sacrificial at the expense of its creative aspect. We might, for instance, see the death on the Cross and forget the Life to which it leads. Altogether, we are in danger of forgetting the *deepest* meaning of the Cross as the symbol of nothing less than the Eternal Self-giving of God which gives being to The All.

Instead of contemplating the symbol of the Crucifix, therefore, we again choose some text as a means of contemplating Divine Love as it really is, the Eternal Self-giving of God which gives being to The All. What Word of Christ shall we choose? The variety of texts expressing Divine Love is almost bewildering. We begin by considering the actual words uttered by I AM Incarnate. But on further reflection these are too laconic to suit beginners. The Lord just speaks of His Love, and that is so far beyond the beginner's experience as yet, that we may well utter His words but experience only human love.

We turn next to the Old Testament, therefore, and here we find

[1] 2 Cor. 5. 16. [2] Rom. 13. 14; Heb. 13. 8.

the ideal sentence for beginners. This perfectly expresses, centuries before I AM's Incarnation, through the prophet Jeremiah's mouth, the ceaseless heart-beat, the in- and out-breathing of the Divine Procession and Return of Love. 'I have loved thee with an Everlasting Love: therefore with Loving kindness have I drawn thee.'[1] The first part of the sentence expresses the inexhaustible Procession of Divine Love which has made and which upholds all things visible and invisible. The second part of the sentence expresses the ceaseless Return of Divine Love by which all things are redeemed[2] and gathered together again in One.

Though there are many sentences in the Bible which are as rich in meaning as this, those that are richer are very few indeed. Before we even begin to let this sentence dwell in us, therefore, we shall do well to grasp its enormously rich meaning as clearly as we can at this stage. The sentence enshrines nothing less than the Eternal Procession and Return, the Outpouring and Indrawing, the Descending and Ascending which constitutes the very heartbeat of The Holy One, in which I AM expresses Himself as The Living All. In mentally repeating the first part of the sentence, therefore, we must try to experience the Almighty and Allwise Love pouring down upon us, and all creation. Or, more truly, welling up within our concentrated, one-pointed, stilled *I am*. For it is here that we approach nearest to the Divine Majesty. And then we must try to feel Love pouring out through us and from us as it makes and upholds all things.

In saying the second part of the sentence we must try to feel that Love, the same Love, drawing us upwards. Or, more truly, lifting us inwards, through the depths of our concentrated, one-pointed, stilled *I am* into the Supreme All-conscious I AM within. For it is here, it cannot be too clearly realized, that we most nearly approach the Divine Majesty. It is here that our *I am* finds union with I AM, or rather dies into I AM. And then we must try to feel that Love pouring out through us, and from us, as it draws all souls and so gathers all things together again in One.

[3]

Having now, rather more fully than usual, in two sections in-

[1] Jer. 31. 3.

[2] Only those things requiring redemption.

stead of one, ensured that our notion of Divine Love is as true as we can make it at this stage, we pass on to our actual attempt to experience Divine Love, thereby carrying our knowledge from the mind down to the heart.

We begin, as usual, by remembering the Lord's Call. 'Come unto ME, all ye that labour and are heavy laden, and I will give you Rest.' We recall our heaviest burdens, and face, accept and renounce them as far as we can. We next turn to the things or beings, as well as the desires or aversions for these, which are the cause of our burdens. And we renounce these as far as we can, too. The chance now comes to us to shed burdens which we have hitherto, quite possibly, not dared to face. These are the burdens arising from our human love relationships. We try to face and accept them, like all the others. Finally, we try to make the hardest renunciation of all, that is, our human love for our beloved, the cause of the heaviest of human burdens.

One may perhaps ask precisely how such a renunciation can be made. How can we renounce something so essentially part of our whole existence, indeed, of our whole *I am*?

The answer is brutally simple. We recall our attachment to our beloved. Then we imagine him or her gone, dead, lost for ever. This must inevitably happen some day, if our love remains merely human. We then imagine the attachment dead, too. This, too, must inevitably happen, if our attachment is the stuff of our love.

Many will, of course, find these renunciations quite beyond their power at this stage, at any rate renunciations that are at all sincere. The first reaction may well be to deny that they have any such burdens. Human though it may be, shot through with desire though it may be, love brings them nothing but joy, they may declare.

The first step in awakening from this illusion is to ponder the Lord's warning that suffering is wholly unavoidable in the world. 'In the world ye shall have tribulation.'[1] Next, we must draw on all the experience of life we possess. And if we possess too little as yet, too little to give us much confidence in it, we must ponder the experience of others. Love may well begin by giving us joy. But we have to remember the fate of human joys, as we did before contemplating Divine Joy.[2] As it is with all human joys, so the

[1] John 16. 33.

[2] See Section 2 of Chapter 5.

very happiness that love brings today is the guarantee of sorrow tomorrow. And the greater the joy has been, the greater the sorrow is likely to be. The burden is on our back already, if only we knew it.

Some may try to dismiss all this as cynicism and, in spite of all that has been said, revive the arguments they used when defending the value of human joys. Their heart will make these appear even more cogent than before. To renounce so noble an emotion as love is morally wrong, they may declare, and even unchristian. But the Lord, in the most explicit language, leaves them no choice. For He clearly declares that this renunciation is precisely what they must carry through. 'If any man come to ME, and hate not his father, and mother, and wife, and children, and brethren, and sisters, yea, and his own life also, he cannot be MY disciple.'[1] He cannot, that is to say, follow ME into I AM. And he cannot ever love as I AM loves.

But when all is said and done, it is doubtful whether the most cogent reasoning on earth can really *ease* these greatest renunciations. We may accept the reasoning with the mind. It is indeed forced upon the mind if we become strictly logical. But the heart will go on protesting. The attack upon our *I am* is undisguised now, in truth, and our whole *I am* protests with all the strength that still remains in it.

Can we soften these protests, and persuade the heart to align itself with the mind in renouncing our human love which forms so great a part of our *I am*?

Ultimately no. There is no anaesthetic for the crucifixion. Or our crucifixion would not be a crucifixion. All we can do, then, is to strengthen our resolution to carry through our renunciations to the bitter end. It will help us to remember the fate of all human joys. It will help us still more to remember how infinitely better we would love our beloved with Divine Love than we do with our own. Our only true help, as always however, is the power that comes to us from contemplating I AM. For so we receive the only power capable of overcoming the world and of enduring the crucifixion. So we receive strength to endure the suffering by which alone all suffering is overcome. So we receive strength to destroy our *I am* which obscures I AM in and to us. As all this

[1] Luke 14. 26. (Hate does not mean 'hatred', of course.)

ceases to be theory and becomes experience, so suffering is truly revealed to us as the work of Divine Love, as the chastening to which I AM subjects us so 'that we might be partakers of His Holiness'.[1]

Perhaps it is only then that we come to believe in our heart of hearts what our reason has told us, namely, that we love our beloved most truly, not with human love, but with Divine Love. Perhaps it is only then that we can really face the destruction of our human attachment to our beloved. For we shall see this as *our* sacrifice for *them* through which we receive power to love them, perfectly, eternally.

Let us assume, then, that we are at least prepared to attempt the renunciation of our human love for our beloved. Once more we return to the Lord's Call. 'Come unto ME, all ye that labour and are heavy laden, and I will give you Rest.' We become as clearly conscious as we can of those burdens arising from our human love. Perceiving as clearly as we can the pain hidden in its joy, we renounce both the burden and its cause. Then we fill the mind with the Word of Christ.

'I have loved thee with an Everlasting Love: therefore with Loving kindness have I drawn thee.'

If the burdens we have renounced, and particularly their causes, are always liable to distract us during contemplation, this is at least as likely to happen in the present case. It is not hard to imagine some of the possibilities. Memories of the renounced affection will force themselves upon us. The image of the one we love may poignantly appear in our mind's eye. As soon as we begin concentrating upon the text, therefore, we may well be overwhelmed with a nostalgic sense of loss, so great that even Divine Love pales by contrast. The Cross at its centre, the sacrificial self-giving which is its essence, may actually repel. Our imaginary colloquy with I AM will stand us in better stead than ever here.

'I have loved thee with an Everlasting Love: therefore with Loving kindness have I drawn thee. . . . I AM not that which is burdened. . . . For I AM above all, and through all, and in all. . . . There is nothing in existence which could possibly burden ME. . . . I AM not that which is attracted by MY beloved; I do not desire MY beloved. . . . It is MY Love indeed which has brought

[1] Heb. 12. 10.

into being and upholds MY beloved. . . . As it has all other things, visible and invisible. . . . And it is MY Love which redeems and draws all things back into MYSELF again. . . . As it does all other things visible and invisible . . . So MY Love, being pure sacrificial self-giving, ceaselessly confers upon all things the Supreme Good. . . . Being absolutely perfect, it confers upon all things MY Absolute Perfection. . . . Be still, then, and experience MY Love in thee as it eternally makes all things, upholds all things in their perfection, redeems that which has fallen, and gathers all things together again in One. . . .

'I have loved thee with an Everlasting Love: therefore with Loving kindness have I drawn thee.'

Ten minutes silence

The silence ends with the usual thanksgiving and self-oblation. 'We thank Thee, O Lord, for all Thy Unsearchable Riches, and especially now for Thy Supreme Gift of Thyself in Love. And so we offer and present unto Thee, O Lord, as far as we are able, all that we are, all that we have, and all that we do.'

[4]

Having tried to know Divine Love with the heart, we now come to the deepest level of knowledge, and the one most difficult to possess, the knowledge of the will. Here our experience of Divine Love becomes manifested *in* us and expressed *by* us. So neither we, nor others, can doubt that we do indeed know Divine Love. That we indeed believe that we have received Divine Love. And that consequently we have indeed received, and do indeed possess, Divine Love. For this streams not only into us, but from us to all beings, and is thus manifestly incarnate in us.

Our first task, as always, is to choose a watchword. One of the most expressive we can choose is 'Eternal Loving kindness'. Another, and perhaps an even more vivid one, is 'Eternal Self-giving in Love'. Each morning and evening at least, and if possible at midday as well, we contemplate Divine Love by letting the Word of Christ dwell in us richly. So we seek the deepest possible experience of Divine Love under the most favourable conditions we can find. By determining to keep the watchword at the back of our mind throughout the day, and to use it whenever a chance occurs, we seek to manifest and to express Divine Love under the most difficult conditions of the hurly-burly of daily life.

If it has been worth while to illustrate the use of the watchword hitherto, this is certainly so here. We shall do so rather more elaborately than hitherto. Anyone with any experience of life is hardly likely to dismiss illustrations of attempts to manifest Divine Love in the world as unnecessarily elaborate. It will be best to begin with a comparatively easy situation. Though even this is difficult enough for any aspirant to union with God, let alone a beginner.

Suppose we see a man maltreating his small son. We go up to remonstrate, and receive an insulting reply. The natural reaction is an impulse to retaliate in kind, and possibly with interest. And if there is a social gulf between the bully and ourselves, pride may also be roused. If, further, we have no doubt of being morally right, so-called righteous indignation may also come into play. The combined force of all these motives produces a strong temptation to reject the watchword as irrelevant in the circumstances. Our first duty here, we argue, is to protect the victim and to teach the bully a sound lesson.

We remember, however, that the surest way to gain *both* ends is to reform the bully. Or he will merely revert to his ways the moment our back is turned. Now force will never reform him. Our contemplation of Divine All-Power should have taught us that. His reform will come about as his self-respect is built up and his conscience is aroused. Eternal Loving kindness, Self-giving in Love alone can do this. For in the degree that he is regarded with Divine Love he is in Supreme Wisdom seen as he ultimately and truly is in the sight of I AM, and is therefore re-created, reformed and redeemed to this state of perfection. By an effort of the will, therefore, we manage to drag the watchword into the centre of our consciousness. 'Eternal Self-giving in Love.' We follow this up at once by hearing I AM speaking to us.

'It is you who are indignant. . . . I, Who AM above all, and through all, and in all, cannot be angry. . . . For I AM eternally serene, and there is nothing in existence to mar MY Peace. . . . I AM eternally All-Mighty, and there is no power in existence to challenge MY Omnipotence. . . . I AM eternally All-Wise, and conceive *all* things in their perfection, including the bully. . . . I AM eternally lovingkind, I eternally give MYSELF in Love, whereby all things are made, upheld, redeemed where fallen, and reunited with MYSELF. . . . If MY Loving kindness, MY Self-giving in Love were to falter, even for an instant, not only the bully, but all things visible and invisible would immediately disintregate, vanish and cease to be. . . . For all these, and all other reasons that are conceivable to man, it is impossible for ME to be angry. . . . I AM Love.'

Difficult though it is to recall the watchword at all under the stress of such emotions, it is far more difficult to keep it in mind. Our will, we are tempted to argue, would be so much better employed in simply suppressing the emotions. If we do that, however, we lose the chance offered by the situation to deepen our knowledge of Divine Love by trying to manifest and to express Divine Love. We shall also have done nothing to reform the bully, or to help his small son. The eternally creating, upholding, redeeming and Godwards-drawing activity of Divine Love will pass us by. As the power of an electric current passes by dead wires. As light passes by closed eyes. We are counted dead before I AM, in the words of the Collect for Quinquagesima. We shall have done nothing to put on I AM, in a word, with all that this implies for ourselves, *and for mankind.*

Let us now turn to a less dramatic, but far more difficult situation. Let us suppose that we meet some attractive person who asks us for help in some emergency. Our courtesy impels us to comply. If the person is young, this impulse may be reinforced with protective other-regard. If the person is defenceless, pity may be yet another motive to come into action in us. All this means that we are strongly tempted to respond from our own resources to the complex attraction of the one in distress.

The beginner may well see no call whatever for the watchword in such a situation, especially if the help asked of him is trivial. Why not let the human impulse have its way? Is it not better to act humanly than to risk not acting at all? Is not certain human kindness better than problematical Divine Loving kindness? Are we not using the one in trouble as a guinea-pig for our own spiritual advancement?

Here again we need to realize afresh that *true* help can only be given *in* and *through* I AM. 'Without ME ye can do nothing.'[1] We may be able to *relieve* some particular need with human kindness. Divine Loving kindness alone can *remove* all needs. The first is an anodyne. The second the only ultimate cure. An anodyne may not much matter where the need is trival. Where the need is vital it may be fatal. And how can we become faithful in much unless we practise our faith in that which is little?[2] Since we can do nothing of ourselves which is truly creative, since we aspire to rise beyond the meaningless activity of churning water, then a single glance lit up by Divine Loving kindness must be worth more than all the world's labour inspired by merely human kindness.

The beginner may well find this another hard saying. But let us suppose that he accepts it and, if only in faith at the moment, is determined to use the watchword in the given situation. (Though he may only reach this point at a later stage in his return to God.) He recalls the watchword. 'Eternal Self-giving in Love.' But whether we are beginners or experienced aspirants, here again it will help us to keep our attention fixed upon the watchword if we imaginatively hear I AM speaking to us.

'Be still, then, and know ME in you. . . . Know MY Loving-kindness in you. . . . It is *you* who are ready to give *your* help because the one in distress attracts you. . . . It is *you* who are responding to attraction. . . . I AM no more attracted than repelled. . . . All creation has no more power to attract than to repel ME. . . . For MY Love has made all things, upholds all things, redeems all things, and gathers together all things in One. . . . If I were to cease MY Loving kindness, who could take MY place in this All-inclusive work? . . . Be still, then, and know only MY Loving kindness in you.'

Let us end our illustrations with the most difficult situation of all. Though it is doubtful whether the difficulty will be recognized by a beginner. And precisely *how* difficult it is only those who have tried to deal with it will know. Let us suppose that we gradually begin to recognize the purely human basis of an old friendship, or still more difficult, of a marriage of many years standing. The charm of the friend or husband or wife has long ago matured into the steadfast attraction of a partner in the pursuit of a common

[1] John 15. 5. [2] Luke 16. 10.

life-aim. Yet that life-aim is something less than reunion with God. Or the situation we are describing would not arise. And because the common life-aim is something less, the partnership, though noble, is something less than spiritual. In other words, being human, it is based on mutual attraction. The attraction is, of course, not any longer physical. Let us give it the highest purely human rank and call it integrally intellectual, emotional and conative. The partners are so wrapped up in each other, or in the pursuit of some common life-aim, that is to say, that their thoughts, emotions and strivings are in complete harmony.

One of the partners now begins to realize that his or her love for the other is purely human. He realizes the 'stuff' of that love to be attraction. He recognizes the innumerable links drawing and binding him to his beloved as desire for the *I am* of the beloved. It would be hardly realistic to speak of recalling the watchword in such a situation. What is more likely is a gradually maturing resolve to manifest the Divine Love experienced during contemplation in *every* situation, including even his humanly satisfying marriage. And, if the beloved does not share that resolve, much clear thought, much courage and still more will-power will go into its maturing. It may be that he will meet here his severest test in his aspiration to reunion with God. It is possible that he will only form his resolution when he clearly realizes that, because it is human, his love for his beloved is less than perfect, less than he would have it be.

But let us suppose that he finally resolves to act on the watchword. 'Eternal Loving kindness, Eternal Self-giving in Love.' If he is wise he will draw all the support he can from his imaginative colloquy with I AM. And, in the early stages at least, he will be wise never to forget that he is surrendering his human love in order to love his beloved with Divine Love. The Cross will remind him of the essence of Divine Love. This is perfect self-giving for the perfect good of the beloved. There is no trace of desire, any more than of repulsion, in Divine Love. For I AM loved, loves, and ever will love before the beloved ever came into being.[1]

'I have loved thee with an Everlasting Love: therefore with Loving kindness have I drawn thee. . . . It was MY Love which

[1] John 17. 24.

brought you, MY beloved, into being. . . . It is MY Love which upholds you. . . . It is MY Love which redeems you from your fallen humanity. . . . It is MY Love that draws you to union with ME. . . . You do not, and cannot, draw ME. . . . It is I Who draw you with the splendour of MY Love, lifted up and manifested upon the Cross.'[1]

No one with any experience of life can fail to recognize at least something of the enormous difficulty of manifesting and expressing Divine Love in a humanly successful marriage or friendship. It used to be a convention in 'the age of chivalry' that romantic love was impossible in marriage. Nothing is ever impossible 'through Christ which strengtheneth' us.[2] Divine Love in marriage is certainly only possible in the power of I AM. Great as the difficulty is, nevertheless it must be overcome, if the ideal of reunion with God is to be pursued *in the world*. As our first chapter has shown, this is man's supreme problem in the present age.

[5]

Summary of the daily exercise

(1) 'Come unto ME, all ye that labour and are heavy laden, and I will give you Rest.'

Two minutes silence

(2) 'I have loved thee with an Everlasting Love: therefore with Loving kindness have I drawn thee.'

Ten minutes silence

(3) 'We thank Thee, O Lord. . . .'

(4) Recollection throughout the day of the Watchword: 'Eternal Self-giving in Love.'

[1] Jez. 31. 3; John 3. 16; 12. 32. [2] Phil. 4. 13.

Chapter Nine

Contemplation of I AM, the Truth

[1]

WE NOW APPROACH the end of the stage in man's return into God with which this book is concerned. Our task now is to reap the fruits of our previous attempts to know various facets of I AM, and try to know Him as the sum of them all. (As well, of course, as of all the other Unsearchable Riches we do not know as yet.) So we make our first attempt to know I AM as the Truth, as the Absolute Reality which is beyond all Attributes.

The truth in its fullness cannot of course be humanly defined. I AM exceeds the sum, not merely of the few Attributes we have so far tried to know, but of all that ever has been, or could be humanly conceived. But as we put on I AM, so *by* and *in* I AM we are lifted up into Himself, and so become capable of knowing the Truth at a depth which is beyond human conceptions and definitions. Every now and then during the course of our Return we therefore need to consolidate progress by trying to unify the Attributes we have tried to know separately into the Supreme Unity that I AM eternally is. Or rather, that I eternally AM, the Truth.

Some may perhaps feel that we have reached an impossible stage in our return into God. That we are, in fact, over-reaching ourselves. If even the Divine Attributes cannot be truly conceived by the human mind, to try to conceive the sum of even a few of them seems hopeless.

But the only alternative is to give up the Return. And whoever does that condemns *himself* as unfit for the Return.[1] We are reminded here again that the endeavour we have consciously embarked upon is the greatest one man can possibly, or indeed conceivably, undertake. For this reason alone it is no waste of time to remember once again its enormous difficulties. The whole subject inevitably strains language to the uttermost.

[1] Luke 9. 62.

We have begun every attempt to know each Attribute by ensuring that our notion, our mind knowledge, of it is as true as we can make it at this stage. We must take the same precaution to ensure that our notion of the Truth is true. (This bit of tautology, suspiciously like verbiage, incidentally, shows us how near we are to the limits of language of any kind.)

When considering each separate Attribute, we always began by briefly reviewing its human travesty, and then tried to conceive it as truly as possible by contrast. We must do the same here. And, perhaps paradoxically, this will be easier than ever before. For if the Truth is I AM, then the human travesty of the Truth is our own *I am*. All that goes to make up our *I am* is thus not *really* true, is not the Truth, is not the Absolute Reality, however real it may seem to us at the present time. Harking back to a point we have already touched upon more than once, we may say that our self-conscious *I am* is not our real, true self. Our *I am* is a travesty of the true Self. Or, as we shall see more clearly and in more detail in the next section, in which we shall try to experience the Truth, we may say that the self-conscious human *I am* is really the sleeping, unawakened travesty of the Divine All-conscious I AM. All of which merely restates the familiar fact that in our fallen human state we distort the Divine Image in ourselves.

We now turn to consider the Truth, I AM. (As far, of course, as we can know the Truth at this stage.) The truth, too, is more easily considered than any of the Divine Attributes. If only because we are so near to the limits of sober language. As we have just seen, I AM is the sum, and more than the sum, of all the Attributes that can humanly be predicated of Him. We already possess a slight knowledge of some of these. Unsearchable though the Truth's Riches may be, therefore, we are safe in saying that they include eternally perfect Peace, Joy, Power, Wisdom and Love. Or more exactly, whatever other states compose I AM, the states of eternally perfect Peace, Joy, Power, Wisdom and Love are among them. And if one were to ask what 'it feels like' to be absolutely Real or True, the answer would be simple. To feel absolutely Real or True is to feel perfectly Peaceful, Joyful, Omnipotent, All-Wise and All-Loving. (As well, of course, as all the other states of being which constitute I AM's Unsearchable Riches.)

This, however, is far less simple than it sounds, even in theory. For I AM is primarily a Unity.[1] Or rather, I AM is The Eternal Supreme Unity. 'The Lord our God is One.' I AM is not, therefore, a succession of various states, as the self-conscious *I am* is, but the eternally Complete and Perfect One. This is not a particularly difficult conception. But the moment we form it, we do so in static terms. We conceive the eternal Completeness, Perfection and Unity of I AM as static. But I AM is Life. His eternal Completeness, Perfection and Unity is therefore dynamic as well as static. Now this combination of opposites *is* difficult to conceive. In trying to conceive the Inconceivable One as He really is, as the Truth, we shall therefore have to recall some of the previous chapters.

In the three previous chapters we tried to know Divine All-Power, All-Wisdom and All-Love. And we tried to know these, it will be recalled, not so much as Attributes of I AM, but as great aspects of the Divine Nature, Life, Activity, Self-expression. As the very stuff, one may say, of the eternally still, yet dynamic, Perfection. Love is the culmination of these aspects. Love is the spearhead, the growing point, the white-hot core of the Divine Procession and Return in which I AM eternally makes, upholds, redeems and gathers together in One all things visible and invisible. Hence we tried to know Divine Love last of all. Our attempt to know Love was really based on our knowledge of Divine Power and Wisdom.

Now this sequence was not accidental. It was imposed upon us by the limitations of human understanding, at any rate an understanding which aspires to be, not merely mental, but experiential, and above all capable of being put into practice. For as a rich man is in a better position to be generous than a pauper, so self-giving in love is more likely to be intelligible to one who is powerful than to one who is weak. The phrase *noblesse oblige* is, after all, intended for the *noblesse* alone. Until we possess some knowledge of Divine All-Power, and have received some measure of this, therefore, it is beyond us to know Divine All-Wisdom in the least degree truly. And still more beyond us is the knowledge of that eternally boundless, unwearied, unconditioned Self-giving which is the essence of Divine Love.

[1] See page 12.

But this cannot be the order, so to speak, in which I AM proceeds and returns. It would be an unnecessary complication to explain why in detail. It is enough to say that I AM cannot need power from which to proceed. For there is nothing beyond or outside Him, to overcome which He needs power. Furthermore, we have just seen that Love is the very 'core' of the Divine Procession and Return. The order in which I AM eternally proceeds and returns must therefore be the exact opposite to the one we adopted in trying to understand His eternal Self-expression. The very first *manifestation* of this, His eternally still yet dynamic Perfection, the very first *step* of His Procession and Return, we may say, is thus His eternal Self-giving in Love. And because He loves perfectly, He is All-Wise. And because He is All-Wise, He is All-Powerful.

As I AM *gives Himself* in boundless, unwearied, unconditioned Love, so in All-Wisdom He *conceives*, and thus All-powerfully *makes* all things visible and invisible. As His Creation reflects His Love, Wisdom and Power, so it is assimilated to Him, so it is gathered together in One. This is the Eternal Descent and Ascent, the Eternal Procession and Return which we have described as the heart-beat, the in- and out-breathing of the One Who is above all, and through all, and in all. So the Completeness, Perfection and Unity of I AM Who is The All, as well as the Source and Goal of All, remains eternally changeless yet eternally dynamic.

This is probably as much as one can profitably say, at this stage, of the Divine Reality, of I AM Who is the Truth. But it is only too possible to agree with all that has been said, yet wonder how even to begin carrying the notion down into experience. Is there not some practical suggestion that can be made for drawing the first breath of this experience, which is supreme in kind, if not yet in degree?

First of all, it is worth remembering that our attempts to carry our mind knowledge down into the heart have never seemed very promising before we embarked upon them. Next, a practical suggestion for a beginning in the present case *can* be made. If we begin trying to experience the Truth as an *unbroken* succession of Divine Love, Wisdom and Power pouring into us, and through us to all things, this is probably as near as we shall at first get to an experience of I AM's Eternally Creating, Upholding, Redeeming and Indrawing Unity. For the rest, we must just become still, and contemplate the Truth by letting the Word of Christ dwell in us. The Word has not failed to teach us before. It will not fail to teach us now, in the degree that we are receptive. As we expectantly present our stilled and one-pointed self to the Truth, like an exposed photographic plate, so we may be sure that the Divine Image will become gradually imprinted upon us in place of our self.[1] Though we know neither the day nor the hour when we are to be visited.[2]

We have not always found it easy to choose a text most suited to beginners. There is no difficulty here. The text we need stands out from all other possible ones. We have, in fact, already quoted it. 'I AM the Truth.'[3]

[2]

We now come to the most formidable task of trying to experience, to feel I AM in us as the Truth, as the Absolute Reality. We begin, as always, by recollecting the Lord's Call to enter into His Rest, that state of Living Changelessness which is the Absolute Reality. 'Come unto ME, all ye that labour and are heavy laden, and I will give you Rest.'

We recall our heaviest burdens. We trace these to our desires or aversions for things and beings. And we do our best to renounce all our burdens, all our desires and aversions, and all the things and beings that attract or repel us.

And now we try to take a further step, as we have tried to do at each attempt to extend the range of our knowledge of I AM. If we can take this further step, we shall enter the last and most difficult lap in the course of our renunciations. We now try to see our entire *I am* as one vast burden.

It will help us, if necessary, to recall once more the dreary ancestry of our burdens. They all stem from our human needs for things and beings, from our desires or aversions for these, from our efforts to satisfy these needs, from the pleasures and pains that accompany all these strivings. What is our *I am*, for all practical purposes here, but a string of all these thoughts, feelings and strivings, and therefore the overall cause of *all* our suffering? These thoughts, feelings and strivings are the very stuff of our

[1] 2 Cor. 3. 18. [2] Matt. 25. 13. [3] John 14. 6.

suffering. And so we make our first direct and explicit attempt to renounce our entire *I am* as the squalid, miserable cause of all our suffering.

In the degree that we do so, not only with the mind, but whole-heartedly, we shall begin to renounce earthly existence altogether. Though we must not deceive ourselves, but clearly understand that this is only the beginning. Our actual crucifixion only begins here. We have yet to endure it to its end. This is the gate to the Fullness of Eternal Life.

Let us assume, however, that we are ready for the whole-hearted attempt to renounce our entire *I am*. How do we actually do so? Unless we make some definite imaginative act, our renunciation may remain merely theoretical. One such act is to imagine ourselves actually losing our hold on life, to imagine ourselves actually going through the process of dying. This is a drastic way of making the renunciation, certainly. But it has the merit of being thorough. The more vividly we can face and imagine our death, the quicker the renunciation will be completed. And if we can face the particular *form* of death we most dread, the end comes quickest of all. But here again, we must not try to undertake more than we can bear. Or some morbid effect may well be the result.

Nor must we linger over the experience. Or here again we may defeat our own purpose. It is impossible now to go into all the ways in which this may happen. All we can say is that we may strengthen rather than weaken our ego, or else throw it off its balance, so that it ceases to be our normal *I am* altogether. In which case it loses its present chance of being transformed into I AM, rather as damaged corn ceases to be capable of bringing forth fruit.[1] We *must* bear in mind all the time that death is but the gateway to true Life, to the Reality, to the Truth. The moment we have died in the imagination, therefore, we must at once fill the mind with the Word of Christ. 'I AM the Truth.'

Nowhere will our imaginative colloquy with I AM stand us in better stead than here. The more we can experience I AM filling the emptiness left by our *I am*, which has just died, the quicker our resurrection will progress.

'I AM the Truth . . . I AM not that which has suffered throughout all your earthly existence and has just died. . . . That was your

[1] John 12. 24.

I am. . . . But I AM He that liveth, and was dead; and behold I AM alive for evermore. . . . I AM not that string of thoughts, feelings and strivings which is now dead. . . . That was your *I am*. . . . But I AM the First and the Last Who Eternally Proceeds and Returns in Perfect Love, Wisdom and Power, making, upholding, redeeming and indrawing all things visible and invisible. . . . So I AM Alpha and Omega, the Beginning and the Ending of all things. . . . Be still, then, and know that I AM God. . . . I AM the Truth.'[1]

Twelve minutes silence

The Silence ends with the usual thanksgiving and self-offering.

[3]

It would be idle to pretend that the last section, or even the one before that, has sufficed to launch anyone but a highly gifted beginner on an experience of the Eternally Changeless yet Living All-inclusive Perfection of I AM. In spite of all that was said, which is not much in view of the subject, most of us will hardly have begun to experience anything very definite. We are all too likely to go on repeating the Word of Christ, for instance, but know little more than *our own* selves feebly trying to feel All-loving, All-wise and All-powerful. Wherever our experience of the Truth may fall short, the All-inclusive Awareness, the All-consciousness of I AM is sure to be conspicuously lacking. And we may well see no practical way of breaking out of the prison of our own self-conscious selves.

Ultimately, of course, each one of us must discover our own way out. 'Ye shall know the Truth, and the Truth shall make you free,' said He Who is the Truth.[2] Only *our* knowledge can set *us* free of ourselves entangled in the world. No one can know for us, or on our behalf. But here again a way found by some of us may help others to discover one for themselves. It will probably be more clearly suggested in a short (and not perhaps very exact) parable than by much theologizing, especially as it lies within the personal experience of us all. It will be best to do so in a section separate from the last one. That dealt with the *death* of our *I am*.

[1] John 14. 6; Rev. 1. 8, 18; Ps. 46. 10. [2] John 8. 32.

The present one may be said to deal with our *awakening* as I AM.

Most of us will have had nightmares at some time or another, if only in childhood. We are familiar with its pattern, from the climax of horror jolting us into wakefulness, to the final state of complete awareness with ourselves sitting up in bed, with the light full on. The climax is often approached by degrees. We find ourselves increasingly helpless in the face of some situation. It need not be particularly horrible in itself, but we seem to be less and less able to cope with it. We try to escape, but our feet seem embedded in treacle. We try to open doors, but our hands are like water. Finally, as we are about to be overwhelmed by the situation, we awake in terror.

At first we hardly know we are awake, or where we are. Our bedroom, pitch dark, is still alive with the nightmare's horror. But as we grow increasingly aware, terror begins to subside. We remember the topography of our room sufficiently to find the electric light switch. The light floods the room, and we at last realize that the horror we have been through was a nightmare, and that we are once more safe and at peace in our bedroom.

When we ponder the experience, we have to admit that it was certainly we ourselves who went through the nightmare. But it was not our normal fully and completely conscious self that was gripped by terror. It was for that reason so much more at the mercy of its environment. It was a self which was vastly more limited, less free than our fully waking self. It was something less than our *true* self, with the result that it was overcome by the nightmare world. The difficulties we went through in that world were real enough. But they were real only to our sleeping self. They were unreal to our waking self.

This common experience, as well as the obvious conclusions that follow from it for our purposes, should help us to enter into the extremely uncommon experience of awakening from our normal human self-consciousness. Nothing is more exactly to the point than S. Paul's call. 'Awake thou that sleepest, and arise from the dead, and Christ shall give thee Light.'[1]

We begin by returning to the point in the last section at which we imagined ourselves dying. Bearing in mind the warning against lingering there, the moment we have imagined our earthly self to

[1] Eph. 5. 14.

be dead, we immediately fill the mind with the Word of Christ. 'I AM the Truth.' We now do our best to identify ourselves, not with our old self-conscious *I am*, which is dead, but with the All-conscious I AM. 'I AM the Truth. . . . I AM the Truth. . . . Not *you* who are dead. . . . I AM the Truth.' We recall the Lord's parable of the corn of wheat which must die before it can grow to maturity and bear fruit.[1] As the green spear shoots from the dead corn, so I AM rises up out of our dead *I am*. We recall our own parable of the nightmare whose difficulties are overcome only by awakening. As our waking self throws off our sleeping self, so the All-conscious I AM ascends from our self-conscious *I am*. Reaching mentally upward and inward, with all the power of concentration at our command, we *feel* after I AM in our depths where He eternally reigns behind, beyond, within, above all, through all and in all.[2]

We find as we seek.[3] Inevitably. For He Whom we seek fills all in all. As the nightmare loses its grip on the waking self, so, as we find I AM our True Self, the world loses its power over us. The world which has hitherto pressed so heavily upon us, through which we have laboured so heavily laden, loses its solidity, its reality in a certain sense.

We may well be tempted here to let it dissolve altogether and to call it illusion. If so, we must resist the temptation. For we are in great spiritual danger. If the world were illusion, there would be no need to seek power any longer to overcome it. Nor would there any longer be room in an illusory world for our ministry. We would shrug off the obligations imposed upon us by our discipleship of I AM.

But the world certainly has power over our self-conscious self. Just as the nightmare has over our sleeping self. It is only in the light of Christ, it is only over the Divine All-consciousness that the world has no power. It is only by the power of I AM, therefore, that we can overcome the world. And it is *only* in that power that we can help others to overcome the world. As we can help another to awaken from a nightmare only if we are awake ourselves.

The surest way of resisting the temptation is not by argument, however, but by resolutely continuing our contemplation of I

[1] John 12. 24. [2] Acts 17. 27. [3] Matt. 7. 7.

AM, the Truth. In putting on I AM, we come to know the Truth which not only sets us free from all error but gives us the freedom of the Reality. We are delivered from the bondage of corruption into the glorious liberty of the children of God, and enter upon our Divine Inheritance.[1]

'I AM the Truth. . . . You shall know the Truth, and the Truth shall make you free. . . . I AM the First and the Last Who eternally proceed and return in perfect Love, Wisdom and Power, thereby making, upholding, redeeming and gathering together all things. . . . So I AM Alpha and Omega, the Beginning and the Ending of all things. . . . Be still, then, and know that I AM God. . . . the Holy One in the midst of thee. . . . I AM the Truth.'

Twelve minutes silence

'We thank Thee O Lord for all Thy Unsearchable Riches, and above all for the Gift of Thyself to us. And so we offer and present unto Thee, O Lord, as far as we are able, all that we are, all that we have, and all that we do.'

[4]

Having tried to know I AM, the Truth, with the heart, we must now try to carry that knowledge down into the will. Whatever degree of knowledge we started with is here completed, so that I AM actually becomes to that extent flesh in us and is manifested in us. As always, we choose a watchword and renew our determination to use it on all possible occasions.

We have hitherto usually found it best to choose a watchword which summarizes in one or two words the essence of the whole text for the month. We may therefore be tempted to make our watchword here simply I AM. But this would be a mistake for the average beginner. For he is as yet unlikely to discriminate very clearly between his self-conscious *I am* and the All-conscious I AM he is struggling to put on. Such a watchword may well cause him to mistake his *I am* for I AM. Then he is in danger of falling into the deadliest of all the pitfalls which beset the Return into God. This is the supreme delusion of being Divine, the supreme blasphemy of making himself God. Whoever falls into this pitfall has

[1] Rom. 8. 21; 8. 17; Gal. 4. 7.

utterly lost the Way. The suffering he must pass through before he realizes this and regains the Way is incalculable. For his delusion may plunge him into the deepest of all hells, the terrible suffering which issues from spiritual pride. The beginner is therefore best advised to take as his watchword the whole text he is using for the daily contemplations, 'I AM the Truth', and draw the very clearest distinction he can between his *I am* and I AM.

So he becomes capable of *deepening* his grasp of the distinction. So his discrimination between his *I am* and I AM grows ever sharper. Nothing more pitilessly reveals the squalor of his *I am*, nor more convincingly helps him to put his finger upon the cause of all human suffering. Thus sooner or later he will recognize his *I am* for what it essentially is, the devil, and with mind, heart and will united in an integral effort, remorselessly determine to destroy it.

If we have found it helpful to illustrate the watchword's use with practical examples before, it will certainly be helpful here. There is no difficulty in choosing examples. The least eventful day brings endless opportunities for using the watchword. We have one, in fact, every time we catch ourselves thinking, feeling and acting in our human self-conscious state. Each is thus an occasion for denying our human selves, and remembering and affirming our true Self, the real Self of all selves, our Lord the All-conscious Divine I AM.

Here again, however, the average beginner will overreach himself if he *starts* by trying to use all such opportunities. They are too inconspicuous for his capacity. The beginner's human self is as yet so little dead, and his resurrection so little advanced, that he is probably more or less content to remain imprisoned in himself throughout the humdrum daily round. He is as yet so little awake that his habitual self-consciousness hardly obtrudes itself as a burden, as long as his life remains uneventful. He is not fit, therefore, to use the watchword where nothing very much disturbs his habitual self-consciousness.

Now one simple way of becoming conscious of some normally unconscious habitual act is to break its normal sequence. We become conscious of breathing, for instance, the moment we are prevented from doing so. We may similarly break the sequence in which we react self-consciously from habit in any situation. We can use the burden created by any self-conscious act, feeling or thought to remind ourselves forcibly of the cause of all our suffering, and to fortify ourselves for the costly effort of getting rid of it. It is on occasions, therefore, when the burden of self-consciousness becomes obvious to us, that we should begin to try to use the watchword.

Many of the examples of the use of the watchword given in previous chapters *could* be used again for illustrations here. But if the daily round is too humdrum to rouse a beginner for the effort of breaking out of self-consciousness, most of these previous examples are too much the opposite for our purposes here. At the stage we are at we should not need anything so drastic to convince us of the curse of self-consciousness.

Let us suppose, then, that we receive some undeserved insult. The immediate self-conscious reaction is anger. This is a burden, plainly. Because we are now more watchful than in the earlier stages of our return into God, we manage to recall the watchword before the human feeling swamps all else. 'I AM the Truth.' Our will keeps this in the centre of our attention. The tremendous significance of this Word of Christ comes home to us. Hardly credible though this significance may seem at first, we try to appreciate the stupendous fact that He Who is the Beginning and the Ending of all things is also our true Self. Our little self, about to burst into indignation, loses its claim to be taken seriously. So does the other little self from whom the insult has come.

As our awakening advances, we become aware of the eternal Procession and Return of our true Self in supreme Love, Wisdom and Power. If the Love, Wisdom and Power which is the eternal heart-beat of The All were to falter, we recollect, not only he who has insulted us, but all other things visible and invisible, would instantly cease to be. He whom we at first saw as an enemy, and then as unworthy of being taken any more seriously than our own little self, now arouses our compassion. This is the beginning of Divine Love in us for him, and we begin to regard him tolerantly, understandingly. So we receive Wisdom to see him at his best. Because we have begun to see him All-wisely, in his essential perfection, we receive strength to treat him in the All-Power of I AM. And as we react to the insult, not with anger, but with Loving Wisdom, so we exert that Power. But though *we* exert it, it is not *our* power but Divine Power. To that extent our one-time enemy is attracted to us. Yet not to us, but to I AM lifted up in us.[1] For Divine Love, Wisdom and Power has begun to pour, not only *into* us, but through us and forth *from* us. Our little self has ceased to exist, and we participate in the Supreme Heart-Beat of I AM who eternally makes, upholds, redeems and gathers together all things. So we are able to do all things through Christ which strengtheneth us.[2] For it is not we, but Christ in us, the Lord all Power and Might, Who is at work.

In such a moment, if only for a moment, if only in some degree, we know even as we are eternally known. One flash of such knowledge, by which all things are made, upheld, redeemed and gathered together, teaches us more than all books ever could. One such flash seems enough for a lifetime, and more, and it is *impossible* not to be lost in wonder, love and awe.

Our previous attempts to use the watchword have taught us that the more deeply our emotions are aroused, the more difficult it is to recall and to act on the watchword. We need not lie down under the difficulty indefinitely, however. Once we have truly begun to recognize self-consciousness as a burden, we can begin trying to use its very intensity for our profit. Rather as an opponent's strength is said to be used in judo. Our emotion italicizes the very thing we are trying to arise from and to discard. Once we come to see the situation in that light, and form the habit of acting accordingly, we can use the very intensity of our passion-inflamed self-consciousness as a fulcrum, as it were, to arise out of it.

We can go still further in this direction. Our parable of the nightmare comes in again here. Most of us will probably agree that we took much longer to awaken from nightmares in childhood than later. The horror of a nightmare had to become quite intolerable before jolting us into wakefulness as children. But as we grew older we usually succeeded in freeing ourselves from the horror a good deal earlier, perhaps at the first hint of its approach. Although asleep, the adult's experience seems to enable him to recognize the approach of the nightmare before he is overtaken by its climax. So, too, we can learn to use the very intensity of self-consciousness to free us from its limitations, before it causes us further suffering.

[1] John 12. 32.
[2] Phil. 4. 13.

Precisely *how* we can use the intensity of our self-consciousness in dealing with our tenacious and resourceful ego cannot, of course, be passed on to another. Any more than any art or skill, least of all the supreme art of discovering I AM, our true Self, which is salvation, can be passed on. Once again we see that *we* alone can *work out* our *own* salvation, as S. Paul so urgently warns us. All one can say is that the more faithfully and resolutely we *watch* our own selves, and *pray* for our true Self, the sooner we shall begin to *use* suffering to overcome all suffering. 'We know that all things work together for good to them that love God.'[1]

[5]

If we ended the chapter with this illustration of awakening from the nightmare of self-consciousness, the beginner might very greatly underestimate the difficulty of awakening to his true Self. For self-conscious existence is by no means always seen as a nightmare. It may be extremely pleasant at times. Those who know no deeper joy are even apt to speak of violent sense experience as ecstasy. Intellectual or aesthetic pleasures are often similarly, though less crudely, misnamed. If we rely on unmistakable suffering to point us to our true Self, therefore, we may seriously delay our resurrection. And should suffering not come our way too obviously, the shadow joys of self-consciousness may delay our return into God altogether. Not that the delay can ever be unlimited. For the shadow joys pall, as we know, and so beget pain. But, as the merest glimpse of All-consciousness once for all tells us, even the least delay in the Return is tragic enough. We must therefore end the chapter by illustrating the use of the watchword in apparently enjoyable situations. We must come to see self-consciousness in its *happiest* form as a state from which to arise. For we know, if chiefly with our minds so far, that even this is no more than a nightmare before the Eternal Joy of All-consciousness.

Let us suppose, then, that we are on holiday, gathering strength to fit us for further efforts. With a clear conscience, therefore, we indulge in whatever innocent activity enables us to relax most completely. This may be walking in peaceful, beautiful country.

[1] Rom. 8. 28.

As we relax in the quiet beauty of our favourite scenery, we feel increasingly at peace with the world. We feel ourselves poised in a serenity, inward no less than outward, which takes the keen edge off all our problems.

Suddenly we remember that the serenity is *ours*, a condition of our self-consciousness, and that we are in danger of being drugged by it as surely as by some sedative. We remember that we shall be as much at the mercy of our problems as ever the moment we lose our temporary poise. It is a conditioned and ephemeral serenity which is no true victory over problems. We succeed in recalling the watchword. 'I AM the Truth.' We also listen to anything else our true Self may say to us in such a moment. All the knowledge of I AM that we possess, indeed, may not be too much to rescue us from the counterfeit serenity in which we are basking. Every one of our colloquies with our true Self is relevant here. All could with advantage be re-read and pondered. We need to remember as vividly as we can that I AM is the Supreme Source and Perfect Archetype, not only of the quiet beauty we are enjoying, but of us who are enjoying it, as well as of the joy itself. That Perfection is, moreover, Eternal and Absolute.

'I AM the Truth. . . . Not you, even though wrapped in the deepest peace. . . . I AM the Beginning and the Ending of all things . . . the Holy ONE in the midst of thee.'

In moments of pain the watchword comes to us as a relief. With some practice it should come to us as a relief, even in a storm of anger. In moments of enjoyment it may well come to us as a bore. Even to one who is well past the beginner's stage. And the greater the enjoyment, the greater the bore is likely to be, like a well-meant word of caution to a youth at the climax of some passionate adventure. It is well to realize clearly, therefore, that we meet here a very severe test of our will.

We shall end the chapter with a review of the most severe test of this kind which the will can possibly encounter. Although a beginner is quite unlikely to meet such a test, he cannot prepare for it too early. The illustration will be useful for other reasons. Nothing could be much more subtle than this matter, and so the same care will have to be given to its study as has gone into its statement.

Let us suppose that we have advanced far enough in contemplation to know moments of true All-consciousness, at least in some degree. Even the few halting references that have been made to this state are enough to suggest that its effect cannot be compared with any human joy. Nor can any language, however profound, however poetical, however extravagant even begin to describe it. Words are as inadequate for the purpose as garden tools are for the repair of a watch. Now it is all too easy to get into the way of seeking such moments for their own sake. Of seeking them, that is to say, so that *we* might *enjoy* them. Especially as there *seems* to be high authority for this. The Absolution at Morning and Evening Prayer, for instance, may be *taken* to hold out Eternal Joy as the fulfilment of human existence. A great Eastern sage is reported (with doubtful accuracy) to have disparaged the ideal of union with God on the grounds that he desired to enjoy the sugar and not to become the sugar.

The temptation to seek such joy for its own sake must be ruthlessly resisted. True religion, whether in the West or in the East, could never countenance this, as the Bible makes brutally clear.[1] The reason is clear. In so far as *we* enjoy such moments of ecstasy, we are not All-conscious but self-conscious. Worse still, we are strengthening the very *I am* that we are trying to destroy. We are giving it the subtlest form of strength that it can possess. We may even be falling into the subtlest kind of confusion between our *I am* and I AM, so that the supreme danger of the spiritual life is upon us.[2]

But we may be proof against the temptation to seek ecstasy for its own sake, and still be in danger. For the ecstasy may come to us even when we do not seek it, simply as an effect, a product, the fruit of a moment of All-consciousness. Let us suppose that the supreme Grace of such a moment has been granted to us. As we emerge from it back into self-consciousness, we may be swept with unspeakable joy. It is possible actually to vibrate with feelings of such intensity as to be almost deprived of consciousness, almost fainting, as though one were a stringed instrument in the hands of a tremendous invisible master-musician. Or the joy may be intellectual. The mind may burst into furious activity, one profound and illuminating thought chasing another in uncon-

[1] Phil. 3. 8; and many other references.

[2] See pp. 66 and 158.

trollable profusion, the whole ecstatic process uselessly incoherent but pleasurable in the extreme.

It is easy to imagine, even without any experience of such ecstasy, how difficult it must be to recall the watchword in such a situation. 'I AM the Truth.' Yet we must recall it and keep it in mind, if we are not to be seduced from the purpose before us, the ultimate purpose of human existence. If we are to press towards our aim of losing our self in I AM and so finding I AM our true Self.[1] For it is *we* who are swept by ecstasy. It is *we* who are stirred with the profusion of thoughts, however profound and illuminating they may be. I AM, the Truth, the Reality, is no more in ecstasy than in agony. No more engaged in thought than sunk in stupor. No more in motion than in stillness. Ever Abiding, ever Proceeding, ever Returning.

'I AM the Truth. . . . I AM the Beginning and the Ending. . . . Be still, then, and know that I AM God, the Holy One in the midst of thee. . . . Abide in ME, and I in you.'

[6]

Summary of the daily exercise

(1) 'Come unto ME, all ye that labour and are heavy laden, and I will give you Rest.'

Two minutes silence

(2) 'I AM the Truth.'

Twelve minutes silence

(3) 'We thank Thee, O Lord. . . .'

(4) Recollection throughout the day of the watchword: 'I AM the Truth.'

[1] Phil. 3. 14.

Conclusion

Brethren, what shall we do?[1]

[1]

OUR OUTLINE of the *stage* in man's entry into his Divine Inheritance, in his return into God, with which this book is concerned, is now at an end. We began by setting this stage in the age we live in. It is best also to end there. Practical conclusions may seem an anti-climax after what has gone before, yet to omit them may even now leave us in danger of *doing* nothing about all that we have considered.[2]

The first point to be noted may be obvious, but it cannot be too clearly realized. This is the length of time we may need to negotiate the stage we have been studying. It has taken some hours to read through. Six months at the very least will be needed to pass through it once in actual *practice*. (Though this makes no allowance for contemplating any additional Divine Attributes, as was spoken of in Chapter 6.) Several repetitions of this six-monthly cycle will be necessary to grasp its deeper significance and to begin to apply the knowledge thus gained in the hurly-burly of daily life. It is better not to speculate as to when the application of that knowledge will become so habitual, so much second nature, or rather nature so much transformed from the human into the Divine, that self-consciousness significantly begins to give way to All-consciousness. It is clear, anyway, that even a gifted and devoted aspirant must be prepared to spend several years in, so to speak, graduating from the stage represented by this book. Most of us will probably take much longer.

Sooner or later, however, we may hope to be ready to reach out for a further stage in our return into God. Which is the next point we must note. Though a beginner may well be thoroughly daunted by the mere mention of another stage. He may feel that the present one is likely to stretch any human being's resources to

[1] Acts 2. 37. [2] James 1. 22.

the uttermost, and recoil from even a glimpse of further effort. He may even ask what further stage there can possibly be. If I AM is the Truth, the Absolute Reality, what else is there to know of God?

I AM is certainly the Truth, and nothing beyond this is possible, or indeed conceivable. Nothing beyond the Absolute Reality can therefore be knowable. But it is all a question of how *explicitly* we know the Truth, I AM. The crudest belief in God, after all, represents *some* knowledge of the Truth. The Reality is known there, but almost wholly from hearsay, and almost wholly *implicitly*. In Chapter 1 we likened theology to a map of the Ascent into God, the Reality. Thus one may say that the crudest 'believer' possesses a correct map of the Reality. He understands, for instance, that all things have been made, and distinguishes between cause and effect to that extent. And even though he sees the Supreme Cause as an old man above the sky, and the Ultimate Effect as the sky and the earth, his map is more correct than that of one who believes in, say, a causeless evolutionary process, however exhaustively he may know its detail. But the crude theist's map is on so small a scale, of course, as to be no more than the barest and faintest outline.

Now the map which we have been using throughout this book is of a far larger scale, and it includes some detail. But it must surely be perfectly plain that the detail is nothing like exhaustive. For instance, we know that the Riches of I AM are Unsearchable. But we have considered precisely six of them. We know that I AM eternally gives Himself in Perfect Love, that He thereby in Supreme Wisdom conceives the Perfect All, and that He thus with All-Power makes, upholds, redeems and gathers together in One all things visible and invisible. But we have considered none of these things except man. Nor have we explicitly considered how any of these things, including man, are made, upheld, redeemed, and gathered together. It should not be necessary to enumerate in what other ways we still fall short of All-knowledge and All-consciousness.

If the aspirant to reunion with God recoiled from the prospect of further effort, he may well despair when he begins to realize how far he has yet to go. Where is all this knowledge to be found? Where is he to find time and strength to acquire it with, to experience it, and to apply it in workaday life?

He must be reminded once more that, in calling him to abide in Him, I AM does not mock him with impossibilities. On the contrary, being Love, I AM calls him to salvation. And salvation means nothing less than to put on the All-knowing, All-conscious One. If he falters or despairs, therefore, he excludes *himself* from I AM. He proclaims *himself* to be unfit for the Kingdom of God.[1]

This may well be cold comfort, however, and something more practical in the way of encouragement may be welcome. First, the aspirant should note that the Bible contains all the knowledge required to enter into All-consciousness. This knowledge is hidden, of course, and is acquired only as the corresponding insight is acquired, and even then only with the help of systematically graduated teaching. But, above all, he should recall his previous experience and remember how, as he put on I AM, so he received power both for a deeper insight into the Bible and for greater efforts to apply his knowledge. It may help here to recall the process by which I AM becomes incarnate in man.

The Word becomes flesh, as we have seen, first by being known with the human mind, then with the heart, and finally with the will. Mind is thus clearly the link, the nexus between human nature and the Divine Nature. Through Holy Scripture, and the theology this has engendered, the Divine Mind speaks to the human mind and through this channel (as through a funnel), facet by facet, degree by degree, God enters man and ultimately becomes flesh in him.

Now it is clear from this that the human mind continually needs feeding with deeper and more exhaustive representations of the Word. Or the transformation of the human into the Divine comes to a standstill, as growth without nourishment, as building without bricks must come to a standstill. (The Church's present weakness in the face of secular knowledge represents such a standing still.) But because the transformation has already begun, because I AM is already partly flesh in the aspirant, his mind is not powerless to accept deeper and more exhaustive representations of the Word, and to apply this knowledge in practical daily life. Further progress into the All-consciousness of I AM is thus not impossible, nor even burdensome, and there is no reason whatever to be daunted, still less to be made desperate by the prospect.

[1] Luke 9. 62.

Even while the aspirant is working through the stage outlined in this book, therefore, he may well be ready to embark upon this more elaborate study of the Word, by the power of the Word having become flesh in him. Which is the sole reason why this further stage is mentioned here at such length. He will then return to books once more. But these will not be the kind of books he gave up when he first began his conscious return into God.

[2]

The use of the first person plural, and the conversational style in which this book is written, both plainly imply the corporate nature of the stage we have been outlining. This implication should be made quite explicit and heavily emphasized. The stage can only be worked through in groups, if there is to be any real hope of success. It cannot be done in isolation. The reasons for this are so fundamental that, as the Preface implied, even 'amateur' contemplatives foregather in groups, often without quite understanding why. Although it is impossible to go into these fundamental reasons in detail here, two of the more important ones need mentioning, if only to overcome the inhibitions against joining groups which many contemplatives, as introverts, suffer from.

The first is mainly pragmatic. The conscious return into God is the most difficult enterprise open to man under any conditions. In the world, in the hurly-burly of workaday life, the difficulty is so great that the aspirant needs all the help he can get from any quarter, and particularly from the mutual encouragement, the fellowship and spiritual support of like-minded people, led by one more experienced than themselves.

The second reason stems from the very structure of man's return into God. I AM is One. *I ams* are many. The Return of the Many into the One must therefore, at some stage, be marked by their spiritual coalescence into supra-individual wholes. It is in this pattern that I AM gathers all things into One. This is why the Church, and true Christianity altogether, is necessarily corporate. It is clear therefore that any genuine aspiration to reunion with God must at some stage be reflected in an irresistible need for spiritual fellowship with other human beings moved by similar aspirations. And whoever does not feel such a need, must realize that he is not yet ready for the stage we are dealing with in this book.

Let us be perfectly clear, then, that this stage can only be negotiated, with any real hope of success, in steady and faithful membership of a group. At first such groups are likely to form wherever a few aspirants happen to be able to meet under the guidance of someone capable of leading them. For various reasons, obvious as well as recondite, they tend to be more numerous in some areas than in others. But ideally, of course, a group should grow up in every parish in Britain, with the parish priest as its leader. In every parish the Church will then be carrying out its appointed evangelistic task on *several* distinct, though closely related, levels. The whole population of the parish will be the field for the general congregation, while the latter will be the field for contemplation groups in various stages of progress. For it is plain that the spiritual needs and potentialities within any single congregation must vary enormously and, once they are aroused, can only be satisfied on different levels. At present only the more common needs are satisfied on the more exoteric levels. The parochial system of the Established Church is thus ideally suited for her tremendous mission of awakening the whole nation to the conscious aspiration to reunion with God.

We saw in the previous section that the stage with which this book deals already adumbrates the next one in which the aspirant reaches out for a still deeper, or rather a still fuller, knowledge of the Word. Now it is likely that some aspirants will find it possible to embark on the next stage even while negotiating the present one. To be more exact, they may find it not merely possible, but *helpful*, to expand their *mind* knowledge of the Word beyond the stage we have reached in this book, but to go on using the method we have outlined here in order to carry that fuller knowledge down into the heart and will. They may need that fuller mind knowledge now in order the better to *experience* and to *manifest* the knowledge of the Word which they already possess. Which is another reason, and the most important one, why this further stage has been mentioned here.

Now it is rather doubtful whether many such aspirants, who are themselves exceptional, will be able to take this further step merely as members of a group such as we have mentioned. They will certainly be working under unfavourable conditions. The mere fact that the deeper and fuller knowledge referred to can only be acquired through a systematic and carefully graded course of instruction points to a closer association with others than membership of a group. This closer association implies a community of some kind.

One may remark that this contradicts the whole thesis of the Introduction and takes us straight back into the past. What becomes of our brave resolve to work for reunion with God while living in the world, earning a living, and raising a family?

The answer is that the community would consist of whole families, not as traditionally of men and women separately. It would be out of place here to go into a detailed description of such a community. Its members might live and work together, say, in running a farm. Or its members might live together, but work separately, each earning his own living. Though the latter would obviously be a mere intermediate stage, since living to rule would in such circumstances be very difficult. For what matters most is that the members should live according to a commonly accepted spiritual rule of life.

The notion of such a mixed community is, of course, not in the least original. Experiments in such ways of life are constantly being made, and not in Britain alone. Their main purpose, however, is seldom to serve the spiritual needs of their members. Because their primary object is expediency, and not the satisfaction of spiritual needs, and because they are not *based* on the spiritual life, they seldom hold together for very long.

Others are based on the spiritual life, and their chances of success are correspondingly high. But at present there seem to be very few communities in existence indeed whose purpose is consciously and systematically to work for the ideal of reunion with God. And, furthermore, by working within the Established Church, to aim at leading the whole nation, and ultimately all mankind, towards the Supreme Ideal. And, above all, prepared to pursue the Ideal with the same degree of intensity and devotion in the world as it has hitherto been pursued in enclosed communities. Is there any such community in existence at all?

The present order of civilization is fast decaying. But although its final collapse is as certain as that of any organism which has ceased to be animated by the purpose for which it came into existence, the end may not be absolutely imminent. Some years may pass before the collapse occurs. But there cannot be much time to *waste*. There never is. It is imperative, therefore, that religious communities be founded at once for families determined to pursue the supreme purpose and destiny of mankind. These communities will need time to overcome the inevitable growing pains of a new way of life, and to become firmly established by the time the present moribund order falls to pieces. These seedlings of the new order will then be revealed as being firmly rooted in the Divine Ground.

[3]

One more practical detail calls for a brief mention. This concerns the social standing of those among whom we are most likely to find the founders of the new order of civilization which is to be rooted in the Divine Ground.

At first sight there seems little to say on the subject. The Lord Himself and S. Paul both knew worldly wealth, power and wisdom to be hindrances to the aspiration to union with God.[1] It ought to be particularly clear to us why this was so then, and has continued to be so ever since. These worldly advantages all tend to enhance self-consciousness, and thereby increase the difficulty of getting rid of the greatest barrier to All-consciousness. The aspirants to union with God in the mid-twentieth century, and thus the founders of the new order of civilization, are therefore most likely to be found among that middle class which is neither perverted by worldly wealth and power, nor by the struggle for the material necessities of existence.

But there is more to be said on the subject than this. For we are concerned here with the British people and their Church. And the middle class of this people is uniquely constituted and is potentially more spiritually fruitful than that of any other great nation in the contemporary world. We should clearly appreciate the reasons for this.

Everyone will agree that Britain is passing through a social revolution. This revolution is almost unique in that it has (so far)

[1] Matt. 19. 24; Mark 10. 25; Luke 18. 24; 1 Cor. 1. 26.

been without violence and that it is in course of producing a homogeneous and almost nation-wide middle class. One of its largest sections has arrived from below. It is freshly self-conscious. It is still revelling in its newly-won power and all the *things* this has brought it. Yet because this power and wealth were won without violence and are now shared generally, their possessors are unlikely to be perverted by them and to abuse them. Sooner or later they are bound to awaken to the empty vanity of these stimulants of self-consciousness. They then come within range of the aspiration to All-consciousness.

Another large section of the nation-wide middle class has arrived from above. This is the former ruling class which has been self-conscious longer than any other class. Some of its members may seek to recover their lost pre-eminence in society by re-entering the ranks of the new rulers. The majority do not seem to regret their lost power and wealth enough to look back in reaction. Perhaps they already realize their empty vanity. They should do so sooner than those who have not been self-conscious so long. They may be among the first to aspire to All-consciousness.

'Whosoever of you will be the chiefest, shall be servant of all.'[1]

Perhaps the former ruling class is best fitted to understand this pronouncement made by the Lord of All, Who is thus the Servant of All. This section of the middle class will then guide a nation which has lost its worldly wealth and power towards the spiritual leadership of mankind.

[1] Mark 10. 44.

Index of Biblical References

Index